101

ONE HUNDRED

AND ONE

Activities for Increasing Focus & Motivation

101 Activities & Ideas

Sue Jennings

101 Activities for Empathy & Awareness
101 Ideas for Managing Challenging Behaviour
101 Activities for Increasing Focus & Motivation
101 Activities for Social & Emotional Resilience
101 Activities for Positive Thoughts & Feelings

101
ONE HUNDRED AND ONE

Activities for Increasing Focus & Motivation

Sue Jennings

HINTON HOUSE Emotional Literacy Resources

HINTONHOUSE

Dedication

For Robert Silman, special friend and mentor, and remembering the fun of working together at the Royal London Hospital.

Illustrations by Matyas Fazarkis.

Published by

Hinton House Publishers Ltd,

Newman House, 4 High Street, Buckingham, MK18 1NT, UK

T +44 (0)1280 822557   F +44 (0)560 3135274
E info@hintonpublishers.co.uk

www.hintonpublishers.com

© 2015 Sue Jennings

First published 2015
Reprinted 2016

British Library Cataloguing in Publication Data

A CIP catalogue record for this book is available from the British Library.

ISBN 978 1 906531 45 4

Printed and bound in the United Kingdom

Contents

About the Author ix

Acknowledgements ix

Introduction xi

    Underlying Developmental Principles xiii

    How to Use this Book xv

    How to Structure a Session xvi

Part One **Focus Games** 1

1	Pass the Clap 1	**6**	Three Tasks 1
2	Pass the Clap 2	**7**	Three Tasks 2
3	One at a Time 1	**8**	The Bakery
4	One at a Time 2	**9**	The Trifle Factory
5	One at a Time 3	**10**	Mess to Order

Part Two **Dice & Card Games** 13

11	Story Dice Actions 1	**16**	Emotions & Actions 3
12	Story Dice Actions 2	**17**	Feelings to Express & Change
13	Story Dice Actions 3	**18**	Actions that Show Feelings & Change
14	Emotions & Actions 1	**19**	Decisions I Want to Make
15	Emotions & Actions 2	**20**	Focus Dance

Part Three **Sensory Distractions** 25

21	Distractions!	**26**	Distracting Smells 2
22	Distracting Sounds 1	**27**	Distracting Smells 3
23	Distracting Sounds 2	**28**	Distracting Sights 1
24	Distracting Sounds 3	**29**	Distracting Sights 2
25	Distracting Smells 1	**30**	Distracting Sights 3

Contents

Part Four Big Distractions 37

31 Distracting Memories 1

32 Distracting Memories 2

33 Distracting Fears 1

34 Distracting Fears 2

35 Distracting Feelings 1

36 Distracting Feelings 2

37 Distracting Disappointments 1

38 Distracting Disappointments 2

39 Distracting Excitements 1

40 Distracting Excitements 2

Part Five Body Learning 49

41 Sequencing 1

42 Sequencing 2

43 Sequencing 3

44 Creative Visualisation 1

45 Creative Visualisation 2

46 Letting Go 1

47 Letting Go 2

48 Switching Off 1

49 Switching Off 2

50 Death by Winking

Part Six Understanding Feelings 61

51 How's My World? 1

52 How's My World? 2

53 How's My World? 3

54 How's My World? 4

55 Family Life 1

56 Family Life 2

57 Family Life 3

58 Family Life Role Plays 1

59 Family Life Role Plays 2

60 Family Life Cartoons

Part Seven Drumming a New Rhythm 73

61 Heartbeats

62 The Heart Tree 1

63 The Heart Tree 2

64 Breathing in Rhythms 1

65 Breathing in Rhythms 2

66 Rhythmic Speech 1

67 Rhythmic Speech 2

68 Rhythmic Speech 3

69 Playing with Rhythmic Scenes 1

70 Playing with Rhythmic Scenes 2

Part Eight Activities I Enjoy: Sports & Games 85

71 Activities I Enjoy: Sports 1

72 Activities I Enjoy: Sports 2

73 Activities I Enjoy: Sports & Games 1

74 Activities I Enjoy: Sports & Games 2

75 Activities I Enjoy: Sports & Games 3

76 An Activity I Would Like to Do: Games 1

77 An Activity I Would Like to Do: Games 2

78 An Activity I Would Like to Do: Games 3

79 An Activity I Would Like to Do: Games 4

80 An Activity I Would Like to Do: Board Game

Part Nine Activities I Enjoy: Hobbies & Interests 97

81 I am Interested in ... 1   **86** I am Interested in ... 6

82 I am Interested in ... 2   **87** Change in Direction 1

83 I am Interested in ... 3   **88** Change in Direction 2

84 I am Interested in ... 4   **89** Change in Direction 3

85 I am Interested in ... 5   **90** Change in Direction 4

Part Ten Using Stories 109

91 Cartoon Tales 1

92 Cartoon Tales 2

93 Myths & Stories 1

94 Myths & Stories 2

95 Myths & Stories 3

96 Myths & Stories 4

97 Myths & Stories 5

98 Myths & Stories 6

99 Journey through the Course 1

100 Journey through the Course 2

101 Certificate & Celebration

Resources

Warm-Up Games 123

Worksheets 131

1   Feelings to Express & Change

2   Actions that Show Feelings & Change

3   Decisions I Want to Make

4a & 4b   Distracting Sounds

5a & 5b   Distracting Smells

6a & 6b   Distracting Sights

7a & 7b   Distracting Memories

8a & 8b   Distracting Fears

9a & 9b   Distracting Worries

10a & 10b Distracting Feelings

Contents

vii

11a & 11b   Distracting Disappointments

12a & 12b   Distracting Excitements

13   The Heart Tree

14   Activities I Enjoy: Sport

15   Sports & Games: Tug of Rope

16   Sports & Games: Swinging & Running

17   Sports & Games: Football & Rugby

18   Activities I Enjoy: Collections

19   Template for Dice

20   Group Contract & Agreement

21   Certificate of Achievement

Story Sheets

Story Sheets 161

   1   A Midsummer Night's Dream

   2   The Shepherd Boy & the Weaving Maiden

   3   The Broken Promise: The Mulberry Tree

References & Further Reading

References & Further Reading 165

Contents

About the Author

Sue Jennings PhD is Visiting Professor at Anglia Ruskin University and an Honorary Fellow at Leeds Metropolitan University. She has been a pioneering influence in the development of dramatherapy in several countries and has established neuro-dramatic play as an approach to attachment that emphasises the importance of early playfulness. She has written many books, a number of which have been translated into Greek, Korean, Russian, Swedish, Danish and Italian. Her doctoral research was carried out with the Temiar people in the Malaysian rain forest, where she lived with her three children. Currently she trains carers in 'Creative Care', for use in their work with older people and people with dementia. She was awarded a Churchill Fellowship for Arts and Older People in 2012/2013.

www.suejennings.com
www.creativecareinternational.org

Acknowledgements

Thanks to all my friends and colleagues in Romania, Malaysia, Singapore and the UK, both for your inspiration and for the ideas that have grown through our play.

Thanks to all my amazing grandchildren who are teaching me so many things, especially computer and phone technology! With appreciation of my creative children and their partners for keeping me younger than I am!

And always, special thanks to Sarah Miles for being a fab publisher.

Sue Jennings
Wells, Somerset
Kuala Lumpur, Malaysia
Zarnesti, Romania
2015

Introduction

This book addresses the issues of children and teenagers who have difficulty focussing on learning and are easily distracted. They often lack the motivation to persevere with tasks and learning. This can result in challenging behaviour (Jennings, 2013) and a lack of positive attitudes towards a learning environment. Another title in this series, *101 Ideas for Positive Thoughts & Feelings* (Jennings, 2014), is a useful adjunct and resource to this volume.

In this book, I build on the theme of change from 'core negativity to core positivity' (Jennings, 2014), as we consider the underlying reasons for lack of motivation in children and teenagers. For many people it feels as if learners are *perversely refusing to learn*, whereas I believe that there may be other core processes that need addressing. It can frequently be the case that they are focussing on something else, rather than lacking the capacity to concentrate! This shift of focus can be due to one or more of the following:

- ☒ Lack of self-esteem and belief in the possibility of success
- ☒ Worrying thoughts and anxieties
- ☒ Abuse (sexual, physical, emotional)
- ☒ Lack of language skills to understand and process
- ☒ Lack of interest or connection with subject matter

I am suggesting that it is possible to return to core processes of physical movement, sound and rhythm in order to build up a new awareness of the self and learning potential. As voice-movement therapist Paul Newham suggests in *The Healing Voice* (1999, p. 12): 'The new-born baby retraces the footsteps of humanity in a few months. For, like the earliest human beings at the dawn of civilisation, babies communicate not through words but through a vocal dance of sound and movement.'

I am also proposing that drama games are a positive means for establishing group communication and cohesion. Furthermore, it is possible to arouse interest in new subjects, ideas and hobbies through physical and creative exploration. How can we help children and young people to flourish?

This work is underpinned by a branch of psychology known as Positive Psychology (see Seligman, 2011), with its emphasis on 'happiness and well-being'. Seligman proposes that we should be 'drawn by the future rather than being driven by the past'. He says:

> The time has come for a new prosperity, one that takes flourishing seriously as the goal of education and parenting. Learning to value and attain flourishing must start early – in the formative years of schooling – and it is this new prosperity, kindled by positive education that the world can now choose. (p. 97)

In addition to Positive Psychology, the approach taken in this book acknowledges the importance of understanding attachment theory (Bowlby, 1965), and its influence on learning. Children who do not have a secure attachment usually struggle with school work and may have difficulties in focus and concentration. It is to be hoped that there are therapeutic resources (play therapy or dramatherapy) available for children and teenagers, but there are often long waiting lists and lack of funding. Many of the techniques here, although not a substitute for therapy, can address learning issues for some of those who are struggling. There are guidelines below to address any 'disclosures' that may be made by participants.

Some children and young people respond well if they feel that an attempt is being made to understand their difficulties, rather than finding themselves simply labelled as non-achievers or suffering exclusion from learning opportunities. Positive Psychology helps to focus on what people *can* do, rather than highlighting their shortcomings.

Perhaps the approach can be seen as 'changing channels', so that negative messages can become positive? The simple act of asking oneself, 'What would I rather be doing?', can be an aid to understanding preoccupation. Many of the techniques in this book directly address the question: 'What is distracting me?' It may be that one of the senses, or worries, or memories are getting in the way of a person experiencing the 'here and now'.

Whatever their experience, it is important that the individual feels valued and that the worth of their own unique contribution be acknowledged. If a democracy of learning can be established, then everyone can find their place within that setting.

Sometimes learning can be enhanced by the 'wandering of the brain': opportunities to day-dream or to imagine something amazing, or wonderful or dreadful, may enable new ideas and creativity to emerge. This process facilitates problem-solving in other areas, as solutions can often be the result of playing hunches or gut reaction! However, many learners get punished for day-dreaming or singled out for sarcasm and ridicule.

Underlying Developmental Principles

There are two interweaving developmental paradigms, 'Neuro-Dramatic-Play' (NDP; Jennings, 2011) and 'Embodiment-Projection-Role' (EPR; Jennings, 1990, 1999, 2011), that form the basis of these practical creative methods with groups and individuals. Rather like the chains of DNA, NDP and EPR create curls and swirls to describe how we think about the creative learning process and how this may be applied with groups (and individuals). Above all, the emphasis is on playfulness and its essential contribution to the health of children and teenagers (Bruner *et al.*, 1985; Sutton-Smith, 2001).

This book illustrates both the underlying theory and the group application of NDP and EPR, and how they can be facilitated for social and emotional growth, particularly with children who struggle with their communication and behaviour. It is about the facilitation of creative involvement to enhance personal and social strengths generally, and focus and motivation in particular.

NDP and EPR are 'value free': they do not rely on a particular school of psychological theory or model of therapy. Being based on detailed observation, they can be integrated into any psychological model or educational practice. However, it must be also stated that developments in Positive Psychology (Seligman, 2011) have continued to influence NDP and EPR, particularly in emphasising children's strengths rather than their deficits.

Neuro-Dramatic-Play focuses on the experience of our earliest embodied development, which commences six months before birth and continues until six months after birth. NDP is characterised by 'sensory, rhythmic and dramatic play' and influences the growth of healthy attachments (Jennings, 2011). It is an expansion of human development during the 'embodiment' stage that commences at birth and continues to 13 months, the most significant growth period for children. Well-being and the beneficial effects of sensory play and physical expression are primarily experienced in the body itself during this period. There is the potential for the greatest impact on the brain–body connection during these months. Whereas the Embodiment stage (0-13 Months) is focussed on the body and the senses, the Projection stage (14 months to 3-4 years) moves beyond the body. There is an interest in objects, toys and materials, building and knocking down. The Role stage (4-6 years) is the time when creative processes are internalised and instead of telling stories through the toys, children start playing roles themselves.

Embodiment-Projection-Role (EPR) is a developmental paradigm that uniquely follows the progression of dramatic play from birth to seven years. Based on extended observations with babies, young children, and pregnant women, it provides a parallel progression alongside other developmental processes such as physical, cognitive, emotional and social.

NDP and EPR follow the 'dramatic development' of children during these crucial formative years for the child's ability to enter the world of imagination and symbolism, the world of ritualistic and dramatic play, stories and drama. Even in pregnancy the mother is forming a dramatic relationship with her unborn child, and the early attachment between mother and infant has a strong dramatic component, through playfulness and role reversal.

Competence in NDP and EPR are essential for a child's maturation, because they:

- Create the core of attachment between mother and infant;
- Form a basis for the growth of the child's identity and independence;
- Establish the 'dramatised body' (in other words, the body that can 'create');
- Strengthen and further develop the imagination;
- Contribute to a child's resilience through 'ritual and risk'(Jennings, 1998);
- Enable a child to move appropriately from 'everyday reality' to 'dramatic reality' and back again (Jennings, 1990);
- Facilitate problem-solving and conflict resolution;
- Provide role play and dramatic play, which in turn create flexibility;
- Give a child the experience and skills to be part of the social world.

Neuro-Dramatic-Play and Embodiment-Projection-Role provide the markers of life changes that are ritualised through play. Literally, EPR and NDP show how life is 'played out' in its first two stages, stages aptly and poetically described by Shakespeare in *As You Like It*:

All the world's a stage,
And all the men and women merely players:
They have their exits and their entrances;
And one man in his time plays many parts,
His acts being seven ages. At first the infant,
Mewling and puking in the nurse's arms.
And then the whining schoolboy, with his satchel
And shining morning face, creeping like snail
Unwillingly to school.

(2.vii.139–149)

How to Use this Book

The expected learning outcomes for working with this method are:

- ✪ Understanding the underlying causes of distraction
- ✪ Recognising underlying emotional issues and attachment problems
- ✪ Discovering new ideas for addressing lack of motivated learning
- ✪ Acquiring skills that promote self-esteem and confidence
- ✪ Creating practical strategies that address school-based issues
- ✪ Finding ways to stimulate new learning and interests
- ✪ Developing an approach for the whole child

The book is divided into ten parts and there are graded exercises within each section which can be used with either younger children, or teenagers, or both.

1 Focus Games (1–10)
2 Dice & Card Games (11–20)
3 Sensory Distractions (21–30)
4 Big Distractions (31–40)
5 Body Learning (41–50)
6 Understanding Feelings (51–60)
7 Drumming a New Rhythm (61–70)
8 Activities I Enjoy: Sports & Games (71–80)
9 Activities I Enjoy: Hobbies & Interests (81–90)
10 Using Stories (91–101)

The first two parts try to catch the interest of children and teenagers and provide safely structured games that use only familiar objects; there are also some ideas for activities that can you can carry out using collections of images or themed packs of picture cards and dice. Parts 3 and 4 directly address the experiences that cause lack of focus, including sensory distractions, memories, fears and anxieties. Parts 5 and 6 have ideas for encouraging physical expression and the understanding of underlying feelings. Part 7 encourages the exploration of rhythm and its impact on brain function. Parts 8 and 9 provide opportunities to explore interests and hobbies, including sports. Part 10 has several approaches to stories and their use to create new thinking and experience.

Group and individual facilitators may use the book to suit their own context, whether in school, community centre or therapeutic resource. Different sections may be appropriate for different settings. Anyone new to this form of active learning could start with Part 1 and build up confidence by 'testing the water'.

Although the book as a whole is written developmentally, progressing from physical and non-verbal activities, to voice and sound, to art activities and then role play, stories and drama, facilitators may choose different sequencing depending on the needs of their classes and group. Generally it is helpful to follow the developmental paradigms of sensory play, rhythmic play, dramatic play (NDP) and 'embodiment-projection-role' (EPR) described above (Jennings, 1998, 2013). This follows the normal developmental stages from conception to seven years, and retraces steps in the progression that may have been missed.

How to Structure a Session

I find the following structure is helpful in bringing some order to a session; it also takes into consideration the 'democracy of learning' and gives time for individuals to express their opinion:

1 Sitting or standing in a circle for introductions, ground rules and feedback from previous sessions, followed by warm-up activities (see Resources, Warm-Up Games, for ideas)

2 Activities (physical, rhythmic, written, or dramatic)

3 Returning to a circle or pairs for sharing

4 The opportunity to record personal experiences in individual workbooks, either by writing or drawing

5 Relaxing with fleeces on mats, perhaps with relaxing music, as a 'cool-down'

These stages form the core of the activities and in practising them from the first session participants will become secure in the format.

Each time the group meets, invite them to sit in a circle, even if only to greet everyone and remind them of basic rules: 'people do not get hurt, property is not destroyed, everyone listens when necessary, and allows other people to speak without interruption or ridicule'. Group members may wish to add more rules (see Resources, Worksheet 20, 'Group Contract & Agreement', for a suggested contract for the group).

Gradually group members are given more choices. Whereas at the beginning the warm-up activities are presented by the facilitator, later on participants can choose and lead their own warm-ups, either in twos or as individuals. Other group members are encouraged to give feedback to support peer learning. The same principles apply to working with individuals, ensuring a gradual transition to more decision-making and choice on the part of the young people involved.

It is also important to discuss with the group the aims of the whole series of activities, which are to:

- ✪ Understand difficulties in concentration
- ✪ Assist people to focus on their current task
- ✪ Allow worries and anxieties to be expressed
- ✪ Provide new interests that will promote involvement
- ✪ Encourage a more positive approach to achievement and collaboration

Resources

I find it helpful to have the following resources available for every session even if they are not always used (they may be needed spontaneously):

- ✪ Large whiteboard and markers;
- ✪ Strong drum and enough percussion instruments for everyone, if possible;
- ✪ A4 paper and card, coloured pens and crayons;
- ✪ A copy (or several) of *Chambers Rhyming Dictionary* (2008), or *Black's Rhyming and Spelling Dictionary* (2003) for younger children; and
- ✪ A fleecy blanket and mat for everyone.

Every group member should have their own workbook for recording pictures, thoughts and ideas, and a personal folder where they can keep completed worksheets and stories. These should stay with the group leader if possible, and then everyone can have them to review and take home when the sessions have ended.

The worksheets and story sheets (see Resources) can be used with specific activities as suggested in the text, or explored freely by leaders and facilitators.

The importance of the warm-up

Every athlete, every performer, makes time for a warm-up before engaging in sporting and creative activities. Some people also think it is helpful to have a 'warm-up for the day' or a 'warm-up to start school activities'. The warm-up is the most important part of the activity session as it helps to focus, motivate, and it channels energy. The warm-up is also linked to the skills and themes to be explored in the session.

In the Resources section at the end of this book there are lots of ideas for warm-ups and drama games. Explore different techniques and encourage participants to have favourites, but also to invent their own.

Every warm-up has three parts: 1) welcome and invitation; 2) discussion and explanation; and 3) physical activity. The activities need to be transparent in their intentions and questions need to be clarified. Reluctant participants will feel no motivation to participate unless they understand the underlying rationale. Examples can be given from sports and media persons and the preparation needed for performance. The body and voice need 'tuning'.

Explanation of core techniques

Freezing

Calling out 'freeze' during a session instructs everyone to stop immediately and listen; it is a core technique that needs to be practised. It could be that the energy in the group has gone haywire and members need to refocus. A 'freeze' can be used when you need to give more information or clarify a query. It can also be used as an active technique: participants can freeze in a particular shape, or scene or feeling, on their own, with partner, or in a small group.

Sculpting

Sculpts are like frozen pictures and are sometimes referred to as 'freeze frames'. Group members can tell a story or present a scene through sculpts: a sequence of postures is held as if group members were statues, with making a contribution to the scene. It is usually simpler to have three sculpts for one story, illustrating the beginning, middle and end. The sequence of sculpts can be dramatised for the whole group as a good basic preliminary to role play and one that is less scary. Soon people realise that sculpts need words, and each member of a group could add a word with their sculpt.

Drumming

I use a drum to call for people's attention, as well as for the rhythm of exercises such as walking. Most people begin to regulate their behaviour when they are habituated to the drumbeats. Drumbeats can help participants become more aware of their heartbeats and relate to their early experience of rhythmic play. Where possible have enough drums for everyone to play, or at least several to share.

Essential cool-down

All sessions need a cool-down period, especially if there is mask work or role play. It is absolutely essential that time is spent 'de-roling' when group members have become engaged in activities. The relaxation with a fleece is a way of returning to normal consciousness after coming out of role.

Potential difficulties

If an exercise seems too difficult, try slowing it down, rather than giving up too quickly. Keep repeating physical routines in order to focus energy that previously was channelled into less helpful behaviours. There is a great emphasis in this work on starting with the body, finding rhythms and developing voice. The body affects the brain and it is the brain patterns that we need to change.

Role work

Many children and teenagers feel silly if asked to take on a role, but usually this does not happen if physical and non-verbal work is done first. It is important for the group to remember that it is not a competition; it is a joint learning enterprise!

Confidentiality

People may share personal material, so it is important to build a confidentiality rule into the group contract or agreement. Personal information stays in the room and is not repeated outside. There is a sample contract in the Resources section (see Worksheet 20, 'Group Contract & Agreement'), or you could create one specifically for your own group. Group members can also suggest ideas for the contract. Sometimes groups need reminding of the terms they have agreed.

Disclosures

Sometimes individuals will share issues of abuse or inappropriate behaviour. This must be dealt with within the guidelines of your organisation or school's safeguarding policy. Similarly, it is now law that every school has an anti-bullying policy, so information about bullying events taking place outside the group must also be reported. Any hint of bullying, sarcasm, teasing or victimisation within the group must be deal with immediately, and group members reminded of their Group Contract or Agreement.

It is important to note that these exercises are not a therapy programme and should not be used as such. Teachers and group leaders need to be observant of the impact of these active methods on group members and advice should be sought if there are concerns.

Part One
Focus Games

Games are well established in education, therapy, business and team building as a method for focussing a group and individuals to a task. The game provides the structure and ground rules and there can be variations, such as degrees of complexity or the introduction of new elements. For example, the first game below starts with the simple passing of a clap, when is then passed by eye contact, and then could change direction or become a double clap, and so on. Group members can suggest their own variations.

It is important to enable the whole group to work together through games and then to introduce small group work and working in pairs. Always present exercises clearly and make sure the instructions have been understood to prevent loss of face if someone has not understood. One way to ensure this is to do a trial run or rehearsal before the game proper. If necessary use a drum rhythm to regulate the game so that it does not accelerate too quickly. The games in this section develop in a more formal way and gradually allow more freedom and decision-making, ending up with real messy play – often a great motivator! Human development moves from mess to order in the play of babies and toddlers (Jennings, 2011), and some people need to restructure their development, temporarily experiencing loss of control as they move in and out of chaos and structure!

Activities

1 Pass the Clap 1

2 Pass the Clap 2

3 One at a Time 1

4 One at a Time 2

5 One at a Time 3

6 Three Tasks 1

7 Three Tasks 2

8 The Bakery

9 The Trifle Factory

10 Mess to Order

1 Pass the Clap 1

☑ Children ☑ Teenagers

| **Aims** | To encourage coordination and focus in the group. |

| **Materials** | Large whiteboard & coloured markers, drums, blank paper & folders, workbooks, crayons & coloured pens, mats, fleeces. |

Warm-Up Invite everyone into the circle and allow time for feedback and questions. Explain the aims of the session, which are to develop skills of coordination and shift energy to accomplish tasks.

Physical warm-up Everyone walks around the room slowly to the drumbeat, then more briskly when the drum beats slightly faster, then faster still when the speed of the drum increases again (no running). Practise walking faster and then slower with the drumbeats.

Activities Everyone returns to the circle and sits on mats. Explain that the group is going to do an exercise to develop coordination and that you will demonstrate it first:

- ✪ Turn to person on your left and clap your hands.
- ✪ That person turns to the person on *their* left and claps their hands, and so on around the whole circle.
- ✪ Now try sending a clap in both directions.
- ✪ Send a double clap in both directions.

| **Sharing** | Continue practising passing claps and encourage group members to think of variations. |

| **Closure** | Draw and colour a hand in the workbooks; relax with fleeces. |

2 **Pass the Clap 2**

☑ Children ☑ Teenagers

> **Aims** To encourage more complex coordination and greater focus.

> **Materials** Large whiteboard & coloured markers, drums, blank paper & folders, workbooks, crayons & coloured pens, mats, fleeces.

Warm-Up Invite everyone into the circle and allow time for feedback and questions. Give positive feedback yourself, both to the group and individuals. Explain the aims of the session, which are to continue to develop coordination and focus, as well as to invite the group members' own variations. Allocate time to learning each other's names.

Physical warm-up Encourage everyone into a sequence: run, run – leap – run, run – leap. Try coordinating the two runs to the drumbeat, followed by a huge leap (compare this to practising for the long jump).

Activities Everyone returns to the circle and sits on mats. Explain that the aim of this exercise is to develop coordination and that you will demonstrate it first:

- ✪ Repeat the sequence of 'pass the clap', making sure that you look the person to whom you are passing the clap straight in the eyes.
- ✪ The clap is passed around the circle in one direction and everyone makes eye contact as they pass it.
- ✪ Then a clap is passed, still making eye contact, in both directions.
- ✪ Two people look each other in the eyes and clap together; repeat around the circle in one direction.
- ✪ Send this eye contact clap in both directions.

> **Sharing** Continue clapping games and encourage group members to think of variations.

> **Closure** Draw and colour another hand in the workbooks; relax with fleeces.

Focus Games

3 One at a Time 1

 Children ✓ Teenagers

Aims To develop sequencing and awareness of others within the group.

Materials Large whiteboard & coloured markers, drums, blank paper & folders, workbooks, crayons & coloured pens, mats, fleeces.

Warm-Up Invite everyone into the circle and allow time for feedback and questions. Give positive feedback yourself, both to the group and individuals. Explain the aim of the session, which is to develop a game about things that follow each other or are done in sequence.

Physical warm-up Call out some physical warm-ups as done by sports people: stretching, skipping around the room, scissor jumps, and so on. If anyone is reluctant, point out that professional sports men and women do this all the time and they don't get embarrassed!

Activities Bring everyone into a standing circle and explain that this game will take some practising.

- ✪ Each person takes a step into the circle, one at a time, going around the circle.
- ✪ If two people step together, the game starts again.
- ✪ The game finishes when everyone has stepped into the circle in sequence.
- ✪ Suggested variations: everyone sits down one at a time, or everyone stands up one at a time.

Sharing Discuss in the whole group how it felt when the exercise got easier.

Closure Draw a circle made up of people's heads in the workbooks; relax with fleeces.

Focus Games

4 One at a Time 2

☑ Children   ☑ Teenagers

Aims   To encourage vocalisation and focus on sequencing.

Materials   Large whiteboard & coloured markers, drums, blank paper & folders, workbooks, crayons & coloured pens, mats, fleeces.

Warm-Up   Invite everyone into the circle and allow time for feedback and questions. Give positive feedback yourself, both to the group and individuals. Explain the aim of the session, which is to vary the one-at-a-time exercises.

Physical warm-up   Everyone walks around the room and high fives all of the other members; repeat, adding names as well as the high five.

Activities   If working with younger participants, or in an SEN setting, check everyone's counting skills (group members can usually count to 10). Everyone stands in circle. Explain that instead of moving one at a time, in this session they will be saying a word or a number one at a time.

- ✪ Each person calls out their name, one at a time.
- ✪ Build up some speed once everyone can sequence.
- ✪ Repeat, but with everyone giving themselves a nickname or a name from a TV programme.
- ✪ Repeat, calling out names and numbers in sequence: 'One, Sarah – two, John – three Darren', and so on.

Sharing   Share everyone's likes and dislikes about the game.

Closure   Illustrate your names in large letters in the workbooks; relax with fleeces.

Focus Games

5

5 One at a Time 3

 Children ✓ Teenagers

Aims To 'embed' sequencing in the brain and body and encourage group dynamics.

Materials Large whiteboard & coloured markers, drums, blank paper & folders, workbooks, crayons & coloured pens, mats, fleeces.

Warm-Up Invite everyone into the circle and allow time for feedback and questions. Give positive feedback yourself, both to the group and individuals. Explain the aims of the session, which are to use one-at-a-time activities for improving concentration and increasing trust in other members of the group.

Physical warm-up Everyone stands in a circle and stretches their hands and arms up, to the side and in front of them. Ask the group to imagine that their circle is standing on the deck of a boat and when the boat sways to one side, everyone sways together. Start the exercise slowly and eventually build up to a storm, keeping everyone's movements synchronised. (This may take several attempts!)

Activities Everyone stands in the circle and creates variations on the one-at-a-time activity:

- ✪ Going around the circle, everyone raises their right arm in front of them, one at a time. Practise to create ripple effect.
- ✪ Repeat, bringing the arm down.
- ✪ Repeat, using both arms up, then both arms down, like a 'Mexican Wave'.
- ✪ Emphasise the way that each person should start as soon as the previous one stops, so that the motion seems continuous.
- ✪ Encourage group members to suggest one-at-a-time ideas and test them out.

Sharing The whole group creates several variations as a combined exercise. Write the techniques on the whiteboard to avoid fumbling and forgetting.

Closure Draw and name a boat in the workbooks; relax with fleeces.

Focus Games

6 Three Tasks 1

✓ Children ✓ Teenagers

> **Aims** To encourage completion of tasks and improve memory.

> **Materials** Large whiteboard & coloured markers, drums, blank paper & folders, workbooks, crayons & coloured pens, mats, fleeces.

Warm-Up Invite everyone into the circle and allow time for feedback and questions. Give positive feedback yourself, both to the group and individuals. Explain the aims of the session, which are to develop everyone's memory and use games to finish tasks.

Physical warm-up A repetition and refinement of the previous warm-up. Everyone stands in a circle and stretches their hands and arms up, to the side and in front of them. Ask them to imagine that their circle is on a boat and when the boat sways to one side, everyone sways together. Start the exercises slowly and eventually build up to a storm, ensuring that everyone's movements are synchronised (may take several tries!).

Activities Give everyone the following tasks and also write them on the board:

- ❂ Jump on the spot twice, clap hands three times, touch four people on the shoulder – all in two minutes (time it and call out 'stop' at the end).
- ❂ Everyone now repeats the three tasks, but works backwards, touching four people on the shoulder, clapping hands three times, jumping on the spot twice – this time in one and a half minutes.
- ❂ Repeat the exercise from the beginning, but now everyone pretends that they are giant aliens and can only do it very slowly.
- ❂ Repeat the exercise, but now everyone has changed to mice – or microbes, or minute aliens – and can do everything very quickly.

> **Sharing** In pairs, play with the exercise with one person pretending to be a very small creature and the other one very large.

> **Closure** Draw a giant alien in the workbooks; relax with fleeces.

Focus Games

7 Three Tasks 2

☑ Children ☑ Teenagers

Aims To further develop the ability to complete tasks and improve memory.

Materials Large whiteboard & coloured markers, drums, blank paper & folders, workbooks, crayons & coloured pens, mats, fleeces.

Warm-Up Invite everyone into the circle and allow time for feedback and questions. Give positive feedback yourself, both to the group and individuals. Explain the aim of the session, which is to play more complex games that further increase skills.

Physical warm-up Everyone is running for a train, or they are creeping past the scary house, or walking slowly to school, and so on. Invite group members to make suggestions.

Activities Everyone stands in a circle:

- ✪ Each person bakes a cake, delivers the cake to someone else and washes up. (They can only deliver to someone who is not delivering themselves.)
- ✪ Repeat the exercise, having two people complete the tasks together.
- ✪ Repeat with four people, but remember there is only one cake so it has to be delivered with care.
- ✪ Can it work with more than four? Experiment!

Sharing In the whole group, discuss the struggles to work together.

Closure Draw a large cake in the workbooks; relax with fleeces.

Focus Games

8 The Bakery

 Children ☑ Teenagers

> **Aims** To focus on a theme, but allow individual motivation to create ideas and actions.

> **Materials** Large whiteboard & coloured markers, drums, blank paper & folders, workbooks, crayons & coloured pens, mats, fleeces.

Warm-Up Invite everyone into the circle and allow time for feedback and questions. Give positive feedback yourself, both to the group and individuals. Explain the aims of the session, which are to encourage theme-based games and develop motivation for thinking up new ideas and actions.

Physical warm-up Everyone runs and 'freezes' (see Introduction, How to Structure a Session: Explanation of core techniques). Repeat several times, then ask the group to 'freeze' in shapes: round, square, tall, small, and so on.

Activities Encourage discussion of all the tasks people might have to do if they worked in a bakery (mixing dough, kneading dough, creating shapes, and so on). Call out the following instructions and everyone responds (usually with lots of laughter). Repeat several times:

- ✪ Baker's Dozen! Everyone works normally.
- ✪ Tea Break! Everyone stops and chats.
- ✪ Boss is Coming! Everyone works very hard and in a focussed way.
- ✪ Strike Time! Everyone stops working and says, 'Mutter, mutter, mutter', to each other in groups.
- ✪ Bread Loving Aliens! Everyone hides under a chair or with arms over their heads, as if they were hiding from aliens.

> **Sharing** Talk about possible variations to the game.

> **Closure** Draw a favourite loaf of bread or a roll in the workbooks; relax with fleeces.

Focus Games

9 The Trifle Factory

☑ Children ☑ Teenagers

Aims To allow messy play and the ensuing creativity!

Materials Large whiteboard & coloured markers, drums, blank paper & folders, workbooks, crayons & coloured pens, mats, fleeces; non-toxic shaving foam, wet-wipes, tissues.

Warm-Up Invite everyone into the circle and allow time for feedback and questions. Give positive feedback yourself, both to the group and individuals. Explain the aim of the session, which is to allow messy play and playfulness.

Physical warm-up Everyone runs and 'freezes' (see Introduction, How to Structure a Session: Explanation of core techniques). Repeat several times, leading the group to freezing in shapes: round, square, tall, small, and so on.

Activities Emphasise that when 'freeze' is called everyone *must* stop or the game cannot continue. Children can wear protective aprons and teenagers old shirts. Say that everyone works in a Trifle Factory and has similar tasks to the bakers in the previous session. Use shaving foam in the exercise, a handful per person:

✪ Everyone Working! In pairs, one person is the trifle and the other is decorating it, using the foam. Change over half way through.

✪ Boss is Coming! Disguise yourself or your partner by making a mask with the foam.

✪ Trifle Competition! Everyone works with great care to create their trifle using their partner.

✪ Trifle Dispute! A free-for-all using the foam!

Sharing Use this time for clean-up, with lots of wipes and tissues. Foam disappears into carpets, but needs wiping off wooden or tiled flooring.

Closure Create a mask that looks like foam in the workbooks; relax with fleeces.

10 Mess to Order

☑ Children ☑ Teenagers

> **Aims** To allow messy play and ensuing creativity!

> **Materials** Large whiteboard & coloured markers, drums, folders, workbooks, crayons & coloured pens, mats, fleeces; thick, blank paper or card, finger-paints in a variety of colours, wet-wipes, tissues.

Warm-Up Invite everyone into the circle and allow time for feedback and questions. Give positive feedback yourself, both to the group and individuals. Explain the aim of the session, which is to allow messy play and playfulness.

Physical warm-up Everyone runs and freezes (see Introduction, How to Structure a Session: Explanation of core techniques). Repeat several times, leading the group into freezing in a shape: round, square, tall, small, and so on. Introduce the idea of 'melting' from one shape into another.

Activities Everyone has thick paper or card and a choice of finger-paints; introduce the idea of 'free painting' and just watching to see what emerges.

- ✪ Suggest everyone paints with eyes closed and then opens their eyes to check what is on their sheet of paper or card.
- ✪ Fold the paper in half and paint on one side right up against the folded edge. Unfold the paper and fold it again the opposite way, and press the painted surface against the blank surface. Unfold it again and reflect on the picture made from the two halves.
- ✪ Fold the paper in half and finger-paint half a butterfly right up against the folded edge. Unfold the paper and fold it again the opposite way, and press the painted surface against the blank surface. Unfold it again and reflect on the butterfly made from the two halves.
- ✪ Everyone has small, round piece of paper, the size of teacup; create a butterfly, as above, and stick all of the butterflies on to a large piece of card or paper.
- ✪ The whole group finger-paints flowers, bushes and trees to complete the butterfly picture.

> **Sharing** Use this time for clean-up and sharing ideas about the group picture.

> **Closure** Create a butterfly in the workbooks; relax with fleeces.

Focus Games

Part Two
Dice & Card Games

Dice and card games provide a structured experience, especially for individuals who may feel that they are completely disengaged from the world around them. When children and teenagers feel 'disconnected', it is very difficult for them to find 'a way back'. Soon it becomes the new way of being, staying away and apart.

These games are tangible, non-threatening and can capture attention. They are fail-safe ways of playing that carry simple instructions and rules. Conventional card packs can also be used before trying out those that are a bit different. Young people themselves can make up new games to play, or be invited to choose games with cards or boards.

Many children and young people feel a greater security if they have some kind of 'prop'. There are all kinds of different card games and themed picture dice available that can help build communication, tell stories, start scenes, encourage decisions, and spark new ideas.

Collections of themed images can easily be made by group leaders using magazines or online resources. You can also create your own sets of six to nine themed action or character dice using Worksheet 19, 'Template for Dice', in the Resources section of this book. Young people who continue not to read can enjoy activities through the pictures on the dice and cards, and this involvement can sometimes lead to a greater motivation for learning to read.

Using sets of themed story dice can have the added advantage of stimulating ideas for creativity and stories. The shape is conventional and familiar, but the varying images on the faces of the dice provoke new ways of thinking. Teenagers can turn onto new pathways by learning to play chess, or drafts, or cribbage, or solitaire. Scrabble is excellent for developing literacy (there are simple versions), while Mah-Jong has a certain air of sophistication!

The dice and card games can also be used to lead into other activities and workshop leaders may want to pick and mix across the sections. For example, several picture dice that lead into a story can later be dramatised as a play; a picture card that shows a person feeling unhappy can lead into storytelling about such a person.

The Leaf Worksheets (Resources, Worksheets 1, 2, 3) provide another way of exploring feelings and actions in a non-threatening way. People can also design their own leaf sheets to express ideas or tell stories.

Activities

11 Story Dice Actions 1

12 Story Dice Actions 2

13 Story Dice Actions 3

14 Emotions & Actions 1

15 Emotions & Actions 2

16 Emotions & Actions 3

17 Feelings to Express & Change

18 Actions that Show Feelings & Change

19 Decisions I Want to Make

20 Focus Dance

Worksheets

1 Feelings to Express & Change

2 Actions that Show Feelings & Change

3 Decisions I Want to Make

19 Story Dice Template

Other Resources

✪ Your own collections of themed pictures about teenage life (from magazines, the internet, etc.)

Alternatively:

✪ A set of *Rory's Story Cubes: Original*
✪ A set of *Rory's Story Cubes: Actions*

11 Story Dice Actions

☑ Children ☑ Teenagers

Aims To encourage focus on ideas and associations.

Materials Large whiteboard & coloured markers, drums, blank paper & folders, workbooks, crayons & coloured pens, mats, fleeces; Actions/Verbs Story Dice (a set of six or nine, created using Worksheet 19, 'Story Dice Template', with pictures or objects stuck onto each of the 6 faces), or a set of *Rory's Story Cubes: Actions*.

Warm-Up Invite everyone into the circle and allow time for feedback and questions. Explain the aim of the session, which is to play with pictures that could be made into stories or events.

Physical warm-up Play physical games that include 'connections', such as Chain Tag or Fox & Lambs (See Resources, Warm-Up Games).

Activities Shake and throw the dice (repeat if you have more group members than dice):

⊗ Everyone chooses one of the dice, with their eyes closed; then opens their eyes and explores the pictures, then creates a connection between two of the six images.

⊗ Shake the dice again and repeat the exercise.

⊗ Repeat again, and share with a partner.

⊗ Create a mini-story with a partner that includes all four of the chosen images.

⊗ Discuss any other detail that needs to be added.

Sharing Each pair tells their story to the whole group.

Closure Draw one picture from the dice in the workbooks; relax with fleeces.

Ⓟ This page may be photocopied for instructional use only. *101 Activities for Increasing Focus & Motivation* © Sue Jennings 2015

12 Story Dice Actions 2

 Children  Teenagers

Aims To encourage sequencing and easy stories.

Materials Large whiteboard & coloured markers, drums, blank paper & folders, workbooks, crayons & coloured pens, mats, fleeces; Actions/Verbs Story Dice (a set of six or nine, created using Worksheet 19, 'Story Dice Template', with pictures or objects stuck onto each of the 6 faces), or a set of *Rory's Story Cubes: Actions*.

Warm-Up Invite everyone into the circle and allow time for feedback and questions. Explain the aim of the session, which is to continue making stories.

Physical warm-up Encourage the group to choose a physical game that involves focus and energy.

Activities Have coloured pens and paper to hand and throw the Story Dice:

- ❂ Encourage group members to take turns to shake and throw the dice.
- ❂ Each person chooses one of the dice and looks at all the pictures.
- ❂ Draw and colour a picture including as many of the dice images as possible.
- ❂ Think about the story in the picture.
- ❂ Write a title for the picture.

Sharing Share all the pictures in the whole group and the titles of stories.

Closure Write the story title in large letters in the workbooks and colour; relax with fleeces.

Dice & Card Games

13 Story Dice Actions 3

☑ Children ☑ Teenagers

Aims To connect pictures to experience, images to action.

Materials Large whiteboard & coloured markers, drums, blank paper & folders, workbooks, crayons & coloured pens, mats, fleeces. Actions/Verbs Story Dice (a set of six or nine, created using Worksheet 19, 'Story Dice Template', with pictures or objects stuck onto each of the 6 faces), or a set of *Rory's Story Cubes: Actions*. Pictures from the previous session.

Warm-Up Invite everyone into the circle and allow time for feedback and questions. Explain the aim of the session, which is to create action stories from pictures.

Physical warm-up Everyone walks briskly around the room and calls out their name, then whispers it, then sings it; repeat.

Activities Give everyone their picture inspired by the Story Dice in the previous session, as well as the dice themselves for rolling again. Work with a partner:

- ✪ Share pictures and dice with a partner.
- ✪ Discuss connections and differences between the two stories.
- ✪ Take elements from each story to create an action story.
- ✪ Rehearse, practise and play with variations and endings.
- ✪ Share with the whole group.

Sharing Discuss in the group the different stories and changes.

Closure Draw and colour one action from the Story Dice in the workbooks; relax with fleeces.

Dice & Card Games

14 Emotions & Actions 1

✓ Children ✓ Teenagers

Aims To encourage connections between simple images, life and creative stories.

Materials Large whiteboard & coloured markers, drums, blank paper & folders, workbooks, crayons & coloured pens, mats, fleeces; cartoons or pictures of young people from magazines or the internet, or a set of picture cards showing young people in a variety of situations with friends and family.

Warm-Up Invite everyone into the circle and allow time for feedback and questions. Explain the aim of the session, which is to develop ideas for stories and situations.

Physical warm-up Invite group members to choose a physical warm-up from the Warm-Up Games in the Resources section.

Activities Everyone has paper and coloured pens. Lay the pictures out, image up, and invite everyone to choose one.

- ✪ Walk around the room as the character in the picture.
- ✪ Experiment with different body shapes that resemble the character in the picture.
- ✪ Write or draw three words that show the feelings of the person.
- ✪ Draw a stick man or cartoon version of the person from the picture onto paper and colour it.
- ✪ Draw a balloon coming out of your cartoon picture's mouth with some sounds or words.

Sharing Show the pictures to a partner and share any personal feelings the pictures bring up.

Closure Draw and colour an image of life as a young person in the workbooks; relax with fleeces.

15 Emotions & Actions 2

☑ Children ☑ Teenagers

Aims To develop personal understanding of feelings.

Materials Large whiteboard & coloured markers, drums, blank paper & folders, workbooks, crayons & coloured pens, mats, fleeces; cartoons or pictures of young people from magazines or the internet, or a pack of picture cards showing young people in a variety of situations with friends and family.

Warm-Up Invite everyone into the circle and allow time for feedback and questions. Explain the aim of the session, which is to develop action ideas from the images and turn them into stories.

Physical warm-up Invite group members to choose a warm-up from the Warm-Up Games in the Resources section.

Activities Lay the pictures out, image down:

- ✪ Each person takes a picture and copies the action of the character in the image.
- ✪ Choose a partner who has a different action and repeat your actions together.
- ✪ Without using words, interact with each other in the 'character' of your chosen people.
- ✪ Discuss the scene and the two characters, as well as any changes needed or wished.
- ✪ Share the scene with the group.

Sharing Discuss with a partner whether or not the scene is familiar.

Closure Draw and colour a cartoon image of young people in the workbooks; relax with fleeces.

Dice & Card Games

16 Emotions & Actions 3

 ✓ Children ✓ Teenagers

> **Aims** To further develop personal understanding of feelings.

> **Materials** Large whiteboard & coloured markers, drums, blank paper & folders, workbooks, crayons & coloured pens, mats, fleeces; cartoons or pictures of young people from magazines or the internet, or a pack of picture cards showing young people expressing different emotions.

Warm-Up Invite everyone into the circle and allow time for feedback and questions. Explain the aim of the session, which is to create relevant action stories about oneself and others.

Physical warm-up Encourage everyone to move around the room as one of the characters from the pictures used in the last session. Repeat, using other people from the pictures, and make up new characters.

Activities Everyone has paper and coloured pens. Spread the images out, face upwards, and everyone chooses a character:

- ✪ Think about who this person might be talking to – or reacting to.
- ✪ Draw a stick image of the two people and where they are.
- ✪ Write below your cartoon any words that might be said.
- ✪ Fold a piece of paper into six squares and draw six pictures for a cartoon story about the two characters, showing what happened.
- ✪ Show and share the story with a partner.

> **Sharing** With partner, choose three actions from each story and show the group.

> **Closure** Draw and colour a favourite cartoon image in the workbooks; relax with fleeces.

17 Feelings to Express & Change

 ✓ Children ✓ Teenagers

Aims To encourage expression of feelings in a safe way.

Materials Large whiteboard & coloured markers, drums, blank paper & folders, workbooks, crayons & coloured pens, mats, fleeces; Worksheet 1 'Feelings to Express & Change'.

Warm-Up Invite everyone into the circle and allow time for feedback and questions. Explain the aim of the session, which is to encourage participants to feel confident about expressing their feelings, especially those feelings that get in the way of 'focus and motivation'; some feelings are difficult to express.

Physical warm-up Jump and run, feeling solid on the floor, focussing on balance.

Activities Each person has coloured pens and Worksheet 1, 'Feelings to Express & Change'. Everyone needs time to look at the sheet and ask questions. Remind people they can draw or write – or both:

- ✪ Suggest that participants colour in feelings they wish to express.
- ✪ Choose colours that fit the feeling!
- ✪ Colour in the second circle of feelings people would like to change.
- ✪ Write any words to fit the feelings.

Sharing Share pictures with a partner and discuss possible ways of changing.

Closure Draw an important leaf feeling in the workbooks; relax with fleeces.

18 Actions that Show Feelings & Change

✓ Children ✓ Teenagers

Aims To assist group members to identify feelings that are difficult to manage and to find ways to change them.

Materials Large whiteboard & coloured markers, drums, blank paper & folders, workbooks, crayons & coloured pens, mats, fleeces; Worksheet 2 'Actions that Show Feelings & Change'.

Warm-Up Invite everyone into the circle and allow time for feedback and questions. Explain the aim of the session, which is to understand how feelings are linked to actions, especially when people 're-act' without thinking through the outcome.

Physical warm-up Practise running, jumping and flying around the room; try repeating this with a partner.

Activities Each person has coloured pens and Worksheet 2, 'Actions that Show Feelings & Change'. Remind everyone they can draw or write or both. Allow time for reading the worksheet and asking any questions:

- ✪ Colour in the leaves showing actions that express feelings.
- ✪ Reflect on any actions that need changing or decreasing in intensity.
- ✪ Colour in the leaves showing changed action-feelings and new action-feelings.
- ✪ Compare the two pictures and reflect on differences.

Sharing Share with a partner and talk about the changes.

Closure Draw and colour one action in the workbooks; relax with fleeces.

  ⓟ This page may be photocopied for instructional use only. *101 Activities for Increasing Focus & Motivation* © Sue Jennings 2015

19 Decisions I Want to Make

☑ Children ☑ Teenagers

Aims To empower group members to make decisions about themselves and their behaviour.

Materials Large whiteboard & coloured markers, drums, blank paper & folders, workbooks, crayons & coloured pens, mats, fleeces; CD of lively music for energetic dancing, Worksheet 3 'Decisions I Want to Make'.

Warm-Up Invite everyone into the circle and allow time for feedback and questions. Explain the aims of the session, which are to encourage members to make decisions for themselves about unhelpful behaviours and to reinforce the idea that everyone has some choice in their actions. Suggest that group members might bring music choices to future sessions for dancing.

Physical warm-up Play CD for everyone to dance, using lots of energy.

Activities Everyone has coloured pens and Worksheet 3, 'Decisions I Want to Make'. Continue any discussion about choices and decisions, and encourage people tackling those that feel difficult or insurmountable; remind the group that they can draw, write or both.

- ✷ Look at Worksheet 3 and encourage questions, reminding people that decisions can be taken in small steps.
- ✷ Colour the leaves to show decisions that individuals wish to make.
- ✷ Draw a set of footsteps and name each one as a small step towards a big decision.
- ✷ Colour the footsteps.

Sharing Everyone acts out their small steps, stating what each step represents.

Closure Write or draw the most important step in the workbooks; relax with fleeces.

20 Focus-Dance

 Children ✓ Teenagers

Aims To show group members how feelings and attitudes can be changed through physical movement that is non-competitive.

Materials Large whiteboard & coloured markers, drums, blank paper & folders, workbooks, crayons & coloured pens, mats, fleeces; large soft ball, music player, CD of lively music for energetic dancing, including choices made by the group members.

Warm-Up Invite everyone into the circle and allow time for feedback and questions. Explain the aim of the session, which is to show how physical movement can help with focus, especially when it is non-competitive.

Physical warm-up Use a soft ball for non-competitive games, e.g., everyone keeping the ball in the air continuously, while passing it person to person in a circle.

Activities Describe the exercise as a music game and, using several types of dance music (including choices by group members), get the group moving:

- ✪ Invite everyone to move as seems indicated by the type of music (include formal dance, African drumming, folk dance, then a group choice).
- ✪ Move with a partner.
- ✪ Move in small groups.
- ✪ The group moves as a whole.

Sharing Each small group shows one sequence to the whole group. Everyone comments on any changes they noticed during the movement exercise.

Closure Write or draw a person dancing in the workbooks; relax with fleeces.

Dice & Card Games

Part Three
Sensory Distractions

There are many different sensory experiences that can stop us from concentrating; this is a common experience and can happen to anyone. We have all been distracted by a passing sound, or the smell of something unpleasant, or an unexpected thought. Usually it is temporary and soon passes; or we may take action such as removing the offensive smell, or going to a quieter room. However, some sensory experiences can preoccupy people to the point of complete distraction so that they lose focus entirely.

The integration of the senses happens at a very early age: some experiences start before birth, and the basic five senses are established in the first few years. Nevertheless, the senses continue to expand and become more complex. For example, food tastes can become more varied, musical understanding can take on several dimensions. However, there are some sensory experiences that can become fixed, repetitive or avoidant, which often happens with children on the autistic spectrum. There are special programmes of sensory integration in this context, and the issue is not addressed in this book.

There are others for whom the senses are associated with certain life experiences, perhaps positive or perhaps negative, but they make sufficient impact to cause diversions. This section encourages children and young people to acknowledge and name these distractions and to explore ways of overcoming them.

Activities

21 Distractions!

22 Distracting Sounds 1

23 Distracting Sounds 2

24 Distracting Sounds 3

25 Distracting Smells 1

26 Distracting Smells 2

27 Distracting Smells 3

28 Distracting Sights 1

29 Distracting Sights 2

30 Distracting Sights 3

Worksheets

4a & 4b Distracting Sounds

5a & 5b Distracting Smells

6a & 6b Distracting Sights

Sensory Distractions

21 Distractions!

 Children ✓ Teenagers

Aims To open up the general topic of distractions that stop us being focussed and motivated for a task; to introduce humour.

Materials Large whiteboard & coloured markers, drums, blank paper & folders, workbooks, crayons & coloured pens, mats, fleeces.

Warm-Up Invite everyone into the circle and allow time for feedback and questions. Explain the aim of the session, which is to think about what distracts us and interrupts concentration.

Physical warm-up Run around the room, then jump, leap, fly, and so on. Shout out lots of words about anything at all very loudly – and then in a whisper.

Activities Use the whiteboard and provide everyone with coloured pens and paper:

- Open a general discussion about lack of focus and inability to concentrate.
- Encourage sharing of specific things that distract people and write examples on the board.
- Suggest that the distractions can be grouped, for example, into sounds or memories.
- Everyone has coloured pens and paper and draws a cartoon or stick person to represent themselves not concentrating (with younger children a discussion about cartoons may be necessary).
- Draw a balloon coming out of the mouth that says something like: 'I can't concentrate because …'

Sharing Share the pictures in the whole group and compare things that are distracting.

Closure Copy the picture into the workbooks; relax with fleeces.

Sensory Distractions

22 Distracting Sounds 1

☑ Children ☑ Teenagers

Aims	To support group members in understanding their lack of focus through being distracted by sound.

Materials	Large whiteboard & coloured markers, drums, blank paper & folders, workbooks, crayons & coloured pens, mats, fleeces; music player, dance CD, Worksheets 4a & 4b 'Distracting Sounds'.

Warm-Up Invite everyone into the circle and allow time for feedback and questions. Explain the aim of the session, which is to think about sounds that may distract us and interrupt concentration.

Physical warm-up Encourage group members to lead dance movement to a chosen CD; make up a game in which one person dances two movements and the group has to copy them.

Activities Everyone has coloured crayons and pens. Each person has Worksheet 4a, 'Distracting Sounds' or Worksheet 4b – allow them to choose either the boy or girl.

- ✪ Encourage discussion of how sounds can be distracting: sounds that are unpleasant and sounds that could possibly revive bad memories.
- ✪ Include great sounds that are enjoyable, and sounds that help to focus.
- ✪ Colour the person on the worksheet.
- ✪ Draw or write positive and negative sounds that are distracting.
- ✪ Draw or write sounds that help to focus.

Sharing	Have a whole group discussion on sounds, distractions, and realistic solutions, such as closing a window or waiting to enjoy certain music until a task is complete!

Closure	Draw or write a favourite sound in the workbooks; relax with fleeces.

23 Distracting Sounds 2

☑ Children ☑ Teenagers

> **Aims** To support group members in understanding their lack of focus through sound distractions.

> **Materials** Large whiteboard & coloured markers, drums, blank paper & folders, workbooks, crayons & coloured pens, mats, fleeces; music player, dance CD, a selection of percussion instruments.

Warm-Up Invite everyone into the circle and allow time for feedback and questions. Explain the aim of the session, which is to think about sounds that may help us concentrate and focus.

Physical warm-up Encourage group members to lead dance movement to a chosen CD; make up a game in which one person dances two types of body shake and the group has to copy them.

Activities With the percussion instruments to hand, encourage discussion of how musical sounds can be distracting and can get in the way of our thinking:

- ✪ Experiment with musical instruments and try out different sounds.
- ✪ Suggest everyone makes a sound at the same time, without listening to anyone else.
- ✪ In pairs, each person plays an instrument and coordinates the sound and rhythm with their partner.
- ✪ In twos or threes, coordinate a rhythm and sound that is enjoyable.

> **Sharing** Discuss the percussion sounds with the group and note if they made a difference to concentration.

> **Closure** Draw or write a favourite instrument in the workbooks; relax with fleeces.

Sensory Distractions

24 Distracting Sounds 3

 Children ✓ Teenagers

Aims To support group members in their experience of sound as irritating or annoying.

Materials Large whiteboard & coloured markers, drums, blank paper & folders, workbooks, crayons & coloured pens, mats, fleeces; essential oils, music player, dance CD.

Warm-Up Invite everyone into the circle and allow time for feedback and questions. Explain the aim of the session, which is to think about sounds that may distract us and interrupt concentration. After discussion, pass around some essential oils for the calming experience of pleasant smells.

Physical warm-up Encourage group members to lead dance movement to a chosen CD; make up a game in which one person breathes in and out very deeply twice, and the group has to copy them.

Activities Use the whiteboard and make sure everyone has blank paper, crayons and coloured pens:

- ✪ Encourage everyone to think about sounds that are annoying to them, such as dripping taps, doors swinging on hinges, and so on. (For instance, you could mention that you find it annoying when young people keep bending drink cans!)
- ✪ Write a list of annoying noises on the whiteboard.
- ✪ Choose two or three sounds from the list and, with a partner, create a mystery story using the irritating sound effects.
- ✪ Tell the story in the group, creating lots of atmosphere.

Sharing Discuss in the group how sometimes annoying things can be changed into something positive.

Closure Draw a negative sound that became positive in the workbooks; relax with fleeces.

Sensory Distractions

25 Distracting Smells 1

☑ Children ◯ Teenagers

> **Aims** To support group members in understanding their lack of focus through smell distractions.

> **Materials** Large whiteboard & coloured markers, drums, blank paper & folders, workbooks, crayons & coloured pens, mats, fleeces; a selection of essential oils, fresh herbs and flowers, and any other pleasant scents, music player, dance CD.

Warm-Up Invite everyone into the circle and allow time for feedback and questions. Explain the aim of the session, which is to think about smells that may distract us and interrupt concentration. After discussion, pass around some pleasant smells.

Physical warm-up Encourage group members to lead dance movement to a chosen CD; make up a game in which one person makes two gestures and the group has to copy them.

Activities Everyone has blank paper, crayons and coloured pens. Have available essential oils, perfumed flowers (not chemical aerosols!) and sweet-smelling herbs. Consider having flower arrangements in the room as a focus:

- ✪ Encourage discussion on smells that are distracting and acknowledge that smell is often joked about (deal immediately with name-calling).
- ✪ Think about unpleasant smells, smells that make the eyes water (mention the effect of allergic reactions).
- ✪ Continue the discussion about smells, positive or negative, that make us think of people or places or situations.
- ✪ Each person creates a positive picture of a sweet garden and perfumes it with oil.

> **Sharing** Put all the gardens on the wall to make one huge garden.

> **Closure** Write or draw a word for a favourite smell in the workbooks; relax with fleeces.

Sensory Distractions

26 Distracting Smells 2

◯ Children ☑ Teenagers

> **Aims** To support group members who are distracted by smell.

> **Materials** Large whiteboard & coloured markers, drums, blank paper & folders, workbooks, crayons & coloured pens, mats, fleeces; a selection of essential oils, fresh herbs and flowers, and any other pleasant scents, music player, dance CD, Worksheets 5a & 5b 'Distracting Smells'.

Warm-Up Invite everyone into the circle and allow time for feedback and questions. Explain the aim of the session, which is to think about smells that may distract us and interrupt concentration. After discussion, pass around some pleasant smells.

Physical warm-up Encourage group members to lead dance movement to a chosen CD; make up a game in which one person makes two gestures and the group has to copy them.

Activities Everyone has blank paper, crayons and coloured pens, and Worksheet 5a, 'Distracting Smells' or Worksheet 5b – allow them a choice of either the boy or girl. Make the essential oils, perfumed flowers (not chemical aerosols!) and herbs available. Consider having flower arrangements in the room as a focus:

- ✪ Encourage discussion on smells that are distracting: unpleasant smells, smells that make our eyes water (mention the effect of allergic reactions), smells we do not like.
- ✪ Discuss smells that we *do* like, which also distract us.
- ✪ Continue the discussion about smells, positive or negative, that make us think of people or places or situations.
- ✪ Introduce the idea that some smells help people concentrate, especially lavender, sage and rosemary (possibly introduce one at a time, over several sessions).
- ✪ Complete Worksheets 5a & 5b and colour the images.
- ✪ Try to perfume the paper using essential oils or other 'containerised' scents.

> **Sharing** Compare the pictures and scents.

> **Closure** Write or draw a word for a favourite smell in the workbooks; relax with fleeces.

27 Distracting Smells 3

☑ Children ☑ Teenagers

> **Aims** To further develop the theme of smells and their capacity to distract.

> **Materials** Large whiteboard & coloured markers, drums, blank paper & folders, workbooks, crayons & coloured pens, mats, fleeces; music player, dance CD, a range of different smells from essential oils, herbs and flowers, white glue, scissors.

Warm-Up Invite everyone into the circle and allow time for feedback and questions. Explain the aim of the session, which is to continue replacing distracting smells with those that help us concentrate.

Physical warm-up Encourage group members to lead dance movement to a chosen CD; make up a game in which one person jumps in two different ways and the group has to copy them.

Activities Each person has coloured pens and blank paper. The group can choose from an assortment of pleasant scents, such as essential oils and herbs:

- ✪ Explain that Roma parents hang rosemary near a child's cot to prevent nightmares.
- ✪ Explain that a sense of smell is our oldest sense, located in the primeval part of our brain; discuss why it might be so important.
- ✪ Share natural herbs and scents and invite comparisons between people's favourites.
- ✪ Draw the plant that produces a favourite scent and create a smell for the page, using drops of essential oil, pressing herbs, and so on.

> **Sharing** In the whole group show and discuss favourites.

> **Closure** Cut out and stick a favourite plant in the workbooks; relax with fleeces.

28 Distracting Sights 1

◯ Children ☑ Teenagers

Sensory Distractions

> **Aims** To clarify why things we see may distract us and suggest diversionary tactics!

> **Materials** Large whiteboard & coloured markers, drums, blank paper & folders, workbooks, crayons & coloured pens, mats, fleeces; music player, dance CD.

Warm-Up Invite everyone into the circle and allow time for feedback and questions. Explain the aim of the session, which is to discuss pictures or sights that might take our attention away from tasks.

Physical warm-up Encourage group members to lead dance movement to a chosen CD; make up a game in which one person creates two different funny shapes with their body and the group has to copy them.

Activities This session needs to be thought through carefully in relation to the school ethos. The main aim is to be able to acknowledge the distraction of 'sexy' pictures; although very normal, this can begin to dominate the thinking of some teenagers:

- ✪ Encourage discussion of visual distractions, whether pictures or people.
- ✪ Acknowledge the normality of visual distractions, but discuss the need to keep this within bounds – attractions might turn into distractions!
- ✪ Share ideas about pictures that might help concentration: posters, photos, especially those showing weather and landscapes.
- ✪ Add pictures of famous stars from sport or entertainment that might encourage concentrated effort.
- ✪ Create a fan page of people whom individuals admire.

> **Sharing** Discuss with a partner the difference between 'fun' distractions and those that take over.

> **Closure** Creative a positive picture in the workbooks; relax with fleeces.

29 Distracting Sights 2

☑ Children ☑ Teenagers

> **Aims** To help participants understand the 'pictures in their heads' that distract focus and prevent concentration.

> **Materials** Large whiteboard & coloured markers, drums, blank paper & folders, workbooks, crayons & coloured pens, mats, fleeces; music player, dance CD, Worksheets 6a & 6b 'Distracting Sights'.

Warm-Up Invite everyone into the circle and allow time for feedback and questions. Explain the aim of the session, which is to understand how pictures in our heads can be distracting.

Physical warm-up Encourage group members to lead dance movement to a chosen CD; make up a game in which one person makes two sorts of funny face and the group has to copy them.

Activities Everyone has coloured pens, blank paper and Worksheet 6a 'Distracting Sights' or Worksheet 6b (allow a choice of either the boy or girl image):

- ✪ Encourage discussion of how our imagination can sometimes distract us; diverting pictures can be unhelpful.
- ✪ Some pictures may be scary, or exaggerated, or sad.
- ✪ Remind people that getting a picture 'out of our heads' can often be helpful.
- ✪ Think of the most unhelpful picture sort of picture to have in your head.
- ✪ Draw and colour it in on the worksheet.
- ✪ Think of something that helps you focus better.
- ✪ Draw or colour it in on the worksheet.

> **Sharing** Work in pairs and share pictures, discussing why they are distracting.

> **Closure** Draw a positive picture in the workbooks; relax with fleeces.

Sensory Distractions

35

30 Distracting Sights 3

☑ Children ☑ Teenagers

Sensory Distractions

Aims To encourage participants to refocus after looking at alternative images.

Materials Large whiteboard & coloured markers, drums, blank paper & folders, workbooks, crayons & coloured pens, mats, fleeces; music player, dance CD.

Warm-Up Invite everyone into the circle and allow time for feedback and questions. Explain the aim of the session, which is to encourage participants to acknowledge pictures that divert them when they are bored, now or in the past.

Physical warm-up Encourage group members to lead dance movement to a chosen CD; make up a game in which one person makes two sorts of arm movement and the group has to copy them.

Activities Everyone has coloured pens and crayons:

- ✕ Open up discussions about lack of concentration and how we cope if we are distracted.
- ✕ Encourage open discussion about what causes lack of interest.
- ✕ Are there ways in which we can change the situation?
- ✕ Draw a picture of a really uninteresting scene.
- ✕ Draw another picture of a very interesting place or picture.

Sharing Share the two pictures with a partner and compare the similarities and differences.

Closure Create a very interesting picture in the workbooks; relax with fleeces.

Part Four
Big Distractions

Activities

31 Distracting Memories 1

32 Distracting Memories 2

33 Distracting Fears 1

34 Distracting Fears 2

35 Distracting Feelings 1

36 Distracting Feelings 2

37 Distracting Disappointments 1

38 Distracting Disappointments 2

39 Distracting Excitements 1

40 Distracting Excitements 2

Worksheets

7a & 7b   Distracting Memories

8a & 8b   Distracting Fears

9a & 9b   Distracting Worries

10a & 10b   Distracting Feelings

11a & 11b   Distracting Disappointments

12a & 12b   Distracting Excitements

31 Distracting Memories 1

 Children ✓ Teenagers

Aims To support participants in becoming aware of distractions and to encourage them to move on from unhelpful memories.

Materials Large whiteboard & coloured markers, drums, blank paper & folders, workbooks, crayons & coloured pens, mats, fleeces.

Warm-Up   Invite everyone into the circle and allow time for feedback and questions. Explain the aims of the session, which are to acknowledge the way people can be distracted by memories and to think about how to move on from this distraction.

Physical warm-up   Everyone has a vigorous 'shake-out', moving as many body parts as possible; then move in contrast, creeping stealthily and silently around the room.

Activities   Everyone has blank paper and coloured pens. Using the whiteboard, encourage the group to give examples of distracting memories:

- ⊗ What does everyone think about when distracted or not concentrating?
- ⊗ Encourage group members to draw or write a word on the whiteboard.
- ⊗ See how many of the distractions are similar or dissimilar.
- ⊗ Are the memories positive or negative?
- ⊗ Draw one memory on paper and colour it.

Sharing   Discuss your picture with a partner and give ideas to control the distraction.

Closure   Write one word of advice in the workbooks; relax with fleeces.

Big Distractions

32 Distracting Memories 2

○ Children ☑ Teenagers

> **Aims** To acknowledge the importance of memories and how they can take over our thoughts.

> **Materials** Large whiteboard & coloured markers, drums, blank paper & folders, workbooks, crayons & coloured pens, mats, fleeces; Worksheets 7a & 7b 'Distracting Memories'.

Warm-Up Invite everyone into the circle and allow time for feedback and questions. Explain the aims of the session, which are to acknowledge the importance of memories and to think about how they can intrude when we are trying to concentrate. Mention that memories can be upsetting, and that it is important to support each other.

Physical warm-up Play a game of 'net-tag': everyone scatters, while one person is the 'net' and tries to trap the others by putting their arms over their shoulders.

Activities Each person has coloured pens and Worksheet 7a, 'Distracting Memories' or Worksheet 7b (allow people to choose either the boy or girl image):

- ✪ Give time to look at the worksheets and ask any questions; acknowledge that some memories can be helpful to our ability to focus (for instance, praise from a teacher).
- ✪ Suggest that the picture is coloured first, while everyone thinks about their memories.
- ✪ Write or draw distracting memories that are negative.
- ✪ Write or draw memories that could be helpful to focus.
- ✪ Encourage the same number of helpful as distracting memories.

> **Sharing** Discuss in the whole group the importance of memories, while acknowledging the need to keep them in perspective.

> **Closure** Draw one positive memory in the workbooks; relax with fleeces.

Big Distractions

33 Distracting Fears 1

☑ Children   ◯ Teenagers

Big Distractions

Aims	To acknowledge that when people are scared it can distract them, but that sharing fears can be helpful.

Materials	Large whiteboard & coloured markers, drums, blank paper & folders, workbooks, crayons & coloured pens, mats, fleeces.

Warm-Up   Invite everyone into the circle and allow time for feedback and questions. Explain the aims of the session, which are to try and understand fears that can distract and how they could be transformed. (This theme is such a big topic that you may need several sessions.)

Physical warm-up   Play one of the 'fear games' from the Warm-Up Games, such as 'What's the time Mr Wolf?', or 'Grandmother's Footsteps'.

Activities   Each person has blank paper, crayons or coloured pens. Using the whiteboard, discuss the theme of fears and encourage suggestions and experiences:

- ✪ Acknowledge that some sharing might be scary, especially if people have been threatened (by bullies, for example).
- ✪ Remind group members that when fears are shared they are much less scary and that everyone is frightened of something.
- ✪ Talk about people who might understand our fears and help us to cope with them, whether in school or out of school.
- ✪ Draw a picture of something or someone scary.
- ✪ Draw a picture of something or someone kind.

Sharing	Show the pictures in the whole group and talk about how to deal with fears.

Closure	Draw a positive picture in the workbooks; relax with fleeces.

34 Distracting Fears 2

◯ Children   ☑ Teenagers

> **Aims** To encourage the sharing of scary experiences and empower individuals as well as the group to find solutions.

> **Materials** Large whiteboard & coloured markers, drums, blank paper & folders, workbooks, crayons & coloured pens, mats, fleeces; Worksheets 8a & 8b 'Distracting Fears'.

Warm-Up Invite everyone into the circle and allow time for feedback and questions. Explain the aims of the session, which are to support participants in sharing scary situations and to empower them in discovering solutions.

Physical warm-up Encourage group members to choose a warm-up game that involves catching and chasing (see Resources, Warm-Up Games).

Activities Use the whiteboard; make sure everyone has coloured pens or crayons and Worksheet 8a or Worksheet 8b (allow the choice from the girl or boy image):

- ✪ Invite everyone to look at the worksheet and share thoughts about fears, and what being fearful feels like.
- ✪ Write words on the board and explain that most fears affect our bodies.
- ✪ Encourage examples of what fear can lead to: tension, anxiety, sleeplessness, and so on.
- ✪ Everyone colours the picture whilst thinking about their own fears.
- ✪ Write or draw scary thoughts and positive thoughts on the worksheet.

> **Sharing** Suggest people share their pictures with a partner and discuss ideas to reduce fears.

> **Closure** Draw a positive picture in the workbooks; relax with fleeces.

Big Distractions

35 Distracting Feelings 1

 Children ◯ Teenagers

Aims	To assist children in understanding how some feelings can be distracting and to find new ways to focus.

Materials	Large whiteboard & coloured markers, drums, blank paper & folders, workbooks, crayons & coloured pens, mats, fleeces; scissors, Worksheets 9a & 9b 'Distracting Worries'.

Warm-Up   Invite everyone into the circle and allow time for feedback and questions. Explain the aim of the session, which is to find ways to refocus when distracted by feelings, such as anxiety, worries, nightmares, and so on.

Physical warm-up   Invite group members to facilitate a chase-and-catch game (see Resources, Warm-Up Games).

Activities   Each person has blank paper, coloured pens or crayons, scissors and Worksheet 9a or Worksheet 9b (allow the choice between the girl or boy images):

- ✪ Show everyone how to fold the paper in four. Draw a person with hands right up to the fold in the paper on the front so that it will still connect with the quarter below when cut.
- ✪ Cut around the person, leaving the 'hands' joined at the fold; unfold the paper.
- ✪ Colour three people as if they have a worry, or something that makes them anxious.
- ✪ Colour the fourth person, giving them a positive face.
- ✪ Look at how the positive face can be helpful to the other, worried, faces.
- ✪ Each person writes a distracting worry on their worksheet.
- ✪ Everyone thinks of an action that helps them focus when they are worried and writes that on the worksheet.

Sharing	Show the cut-outs in the whole group and talk about changing negative feelings.

Closure	Draw stick people in the workbooks; relax with fleeces.

Big Distractions

36 Distracting Feelings 2

○ Children ☑ Teenagers

> **Aims** To encourage emotional literacy, so that people increase their vocabulary and understanding of feelings.

> **Materials** Large whiteboard & coloured markers, drums, blank paper & folders, workbooks, crayons & coloured pens, mats, fleeces; Worksheets 10a & 10b 'Distracted Feelings'.

Warm-Up Invite everyone into the circle and allow time for feedback and questions. Explain the aim of the session, which is to understand feelings that can distract and what may cause them.

Physical warm-up Encourage group members to develop a warm-up that does not involve words.

Activities Coloured pens or crayons for each person and Worksheet 10a or Worksheet 10b (allow a choice between the images):

- ✪ Discuss the worksheet and worries that distract.
- ✪ Encourage group members to write or draw words on the whiteboard: perhaps they are angry, sad, worried, confused, for example?
- ✪ Colour the picture on the worksheet while thinking about distracting feelings.
- ✪ Write or draw feelings are distracting and also feelings that help to focus.

> **Sharing** Discuss the pictures with the whole group and compare suggestions to help people focus.

> **Closure** Create a fun and positive picture in the workbooks; relax with fleeces.

Big Distractions

Distracting Disappointments 1

☑ Children ☑ Teenagers

Big Distractions

> **Aims** To support children in dealing with disappointments and in moving on, where possible.

> **Materials** Large whiteboard & coloured markers, drums, blank paper & folders, workbooks, crayons & coloured pens, mats, fleeces.

Warm-Up Invite everyone into the circle and allow time for feedback and questions. Explain the aims of the session, which are how to express disappointments about things that happen (or do not happen) in life and to discover how to move forward.

Physical warm-up Everyone takes it in turn to facilitate a favourite warm up game.

Activities Use the whiteboard to facilitate discussion and then lead the group into physical movement:

- ✪ Discuss what sorts of things we are disappointed about: something we hoped to be given or to achieve, for example.
- ✪ Write the ideas that come up on whiteboard.
- ✪ Encourage everyone to spread around the room and have a 'shake-out'.
- ✪ Make a body sculpture of 'disappointment', using partners; then change roles.
- ✪ Give the sculpture one word and say that word quietly and then loudly; change roles.

> **Sharing** Talk to a partner how it felt to experience these feelings.

> **Closure** Write one achievement in the workbooks; relax with fleeces.

38 Distracting Disappointments 2

 Children ✓ Teenagers

Aims To refocus attention on a distraction and to understand it through role play.

Materials Large whiteboard & coloured markers, drums, blank paper & folders, workbooks, crayons & coloured pens, mats, fleeces; Worksheets 11a & 11b 'Distracting Disappointments'.

Warm-Up Invite everyone into the circle and allow time for feedback and questions. Explain the aims of the session, which are to talk about disappointments, acknowledge the associated feelings and to learn how move on.

Physical warm-up Encourage group members, particularly those who have experienced several disappointments, to lead a game.

Activities Each person has Worksheet 11a or Worksheet 11b (allow a choice between the boy and girl images). Using the whiteboard and markers, encourage everyone to:

- ✪ Suggest disappointments and write them on the board.
- ✪ Discuss the similarities and differences between the experiences.
- ✪ Write a personal disappointment on the worksheet.
- ✪ Write a positive wish that helps you focus on the worksheet.
- ✪ Walk around the room in a body that is 'disappointed'; then transform the disappointment to celebration.
- ✪ In pairs, create a mini role play without words in which someone receives disappointing news; swap roles.
- ✪ Play the scene with words; swap roles.

Sharing Show the scenes to other group members and talk about feelings of disappointment.

Closure Draw and colour a star in the workbooks; relax with fleeces.

Big Distractions

39 Distracting Excitements 1

 Children ✓ Teenagers

Aims To support participants to understand how exciting memories or thoughts of future events can distract us from the here and now.

Materials Large whiteboard & coloured markers, drums, blank paper & folders, workbooks, crayons & coloured pens, mats, fleeces; Worksheets 12a & 12b 'Distracting Excitements'.

Warm-Up Invite everyone into the circle and allow time for feedback and questions. Explain the aims of the session which are to acknowledge how people get distracted by exciting events, and how to move on.

Physical warm-up Everyone makes a vigorous 'shake-out' moving as many body-parts as possible; contrast with moving stealthily round the room without making a sound. Then start with stealth and get more and more energetic. Jump and Dance for an exciting event.

Activities Each person has Worksheet 12a or 12b (allow a choice between the girl and boy images). Using the white board encourage everyone to think of examples of distracting exciting events:

- ✪ What positive events in the past do we remember with excitement?
- ✪ Think about whether we feel life was better in the past than now, which words describe the thoughts?
- ✪ Compare whether the words on the board are very similar or different.
- ✪ On the worksheet write one exciting memory that is a distraction, and one that helps to focus.
- ✪ Imagine the memory is part of a play about your life, and all events have to come to an end.

Sharing Discuss the exciting memory with a partner and think of ways to stop it being a distraction.

Closure Write one word of advice in work book; relax with fleece.

Big Distractions

40 Distracting Excitements 2

 Children ✓ Teenagers

Aims To understand the difficulties of staying in the present when there are exciting events in the future.

Materials Large whiteboard & coloured markers, drums, blank paper & folders, workbooks, crayons & coloured pens, mats, fleeces; scissors, glue or sticky tape. Worksheet 19 'Template for Dice' (3 for each person)

Warm-Up Invite everyone into the circle and allow time for feedback and questions. Explain the aims of the session which are to acknowledge the importance of positive events but how they can intrude when we are trying to concentrate.

Physical warm-up Play a game of 'net-tag' where everyone runs away, one person is the net and tries to trap someone else by putting their arms over their shoulders.

Activities Coloured pens, 3 copies of Worksheet 19 per person, scissors, glue or sticky tape

- ⊗ Each person has three dice templates and colours each one with a different colour to represent the past, present and future
- ⊗ Give time to make simple little boxes with open lids from the worksheets, by folding and sticking (younger children may need help)
- ⊗ Suggest that each box represents something exciting, and to think about three exciting thoughts.
- ⊗ Write or draw events on small pieces of paper for past, present and future.
- ⊗ Place the events in the appropriate box.

Sharing Discuss ideas with a partner and compare the boxes.

Closure Draw one exciting event in workbook; relax with fleece.

Big Distractions

Part Five
Body Learning

Early security and attachment is established through bodily contact between mother (or carer) and infant. The attachment relationship includes sensory exploration and expression, and the infant slowly develops a sense of 'body self' and later a body image. Children who do not have this close physical relationship often grow up feeling disorientated or uncoordinated and clumsy. Since it is the body that feeds the brain both in childhood and throughout life, it is easy to see how children and teenagers experiencing bodily neglect can shut down their feelings and have difficulties with concentration and motivation.

Bodies are the primary means of learning and all other learning is secondary. The body holds memories of earlier experience, which can result in bodies feeling 'frozen' or 'out of control' or yearning for comfort. Singing games in infancy can teach sequencing and order, and sports of all kinds help to integrate physical coordination in small and large movements.

The techniques in this section address issues of sequencing, and the use of creative visualisation enables participants to let go of unhelpful patterns of movement and to use the imagination to create a 'safe place'. These techniques need to be conducted in a calm atmosphere with no interruptions.

Activities

41 Sequencing 1

42 Sequencing 2

43 Sequencing 3

44 Creative Visualisation 1

45 Creative Visualisation 2

46 Letting Go 1

47 Letting Go 2

48 Switching Off 1

49 Switching Off 2

50 Death by Winking

Body Learning

41 Sequencing 1

☑ Children ☑ Teenagers

> **Aims** To encourage participants to develop coordinated movements that will assist them to concentrate.

> **Materials** Large whiteboard & coloured markers, drums, blank paper & folders, workbooks, crayons & coloured pens, mats, fleeces; music player and choices of current dance music.

Warm-Up Invite everyone into the circle and allow time for feedback and questions. Explain the aim of the session, which is to focus on group members' physical skills and development. (And yes, that includes hip-hop dance, or any other style they enjoy!)

Physical warm-up Group members choose pieces of music and move around the room to these.

Activities Continue the warm-up and develop variations:

- ✪ Continue dancing, but at the aliens' party (or the giants' or fairies' parties).
- ✪ Improvise new sequences to alternate with the themed movements.
- ✪ Repeat the sequences and allow improvisation.
- ✪ Everyone tries to make a continuous sequence of dance, with one person starting as soon as the other has stopped.
- ✪ Everyone tries to make it as LARGE as they can.

> **Sharing** Discuss in the whole group how to make a festival of pop dance.

> **Closure** Draw the shape of a dance movement in the workbooks; relax with fleeces.

Body Learning

42 Sequencing 2

 Children ✓ Teenagers

| Aims | To empower participants in creating their own solutions through sequenced movement and improvisation. |

| Materials | Large whiteboard & coloured markers, drums, blank paper & folders, workbooks, crayons & coloured pens, mats, fleeces, music player and choices of current dance music. |

Warm-Up   Invite everyone into the circle and allow time for feedback and questions. Explain the aim of the session, which is to encourage people to think of their own possible solutions.

Physical warm-up   Encourage group members to lead dance movements to chosen music; make up a game in which one person makes two different wrist and elbow movements and the group has to copy them, each person in turn adding their own movements.

Activities   Continue the warm-up, remembering and reusing the range of movements danced while moving to music chosen by group members:

- ✪ In pairs, sequence some of the movements to form a continuous short dance to the music.
- ✪ Join two pairs together and connect movements for a small group dance that can be repeated.
- ✪ Suggest that this set dance can alternate with improvised movement.
- ✪ Repeat the sequences and allow improvisation.
- ✪ Encourage groups to create a continuous dance, one after the other, by sensing (rather than observing) when the previous dance has ended and the next should begin.

| Sharing | Discuss in small groups your preferences for structured sequence and improvisation. |

| Closure | Draw the shape of a dance movement in the workbooks; relax with fleeces. |

Body Learning

43 Sequencing 3

☑ Children ☑ Teenagers

> **Aims** To encourage participants to create a celebration of their movement work.

> **Materials** Large whiteboard & coloured markers, drums, blank paper & folders, workbooks, crayons & coloured pens, mats, fleeces; music player and music.

Warm-Up Invite everyone into the circle and allow time for feedback and questions. Explain the aims of the session, which are to develop dance skills and to hold a celebration or festival.

Physical warm-up Encourage group members to lead dance movement to their own choices of music.

Activities Everyone has coloured pens or crayons and paper. Build on the previous session, in which group members developed their own dances of repetition and improvisation:

- ✪ Each small group of two or more pairs shows their dance to the whole group.
- ✪ The groups should make decisions about the music they will dance to.
- ✪ Each group creates a poster for their dance.
- ✪ The whole group decides how the festival will start and end.
- ✪ Start the show!

> **Sharing** Give positive feedback to everyone.

> **Closure** Draw movement shapes in the workbooks; relax with fleeces.

Body Learning

44 Creative Visualisation 1

 Children ✓ Teenagers

Aims To encourage participants to learn how to refocus their attention by using their imagination.

Materials Large whiteboard & coloured markers, drums, blank paper & folders, workbooks, crayons & coloured pens, mats, fleeces.

Warm-Up Invite everyone into the circle and allow time for feedback and questions. Explain the aim of the session, which is to practice relaxation and focussing.

Physical warm-up Everyone lies on the floor and stretches and yawns several times.

Activities Each person lies on their own mat with a fleece nearby:

- ⊗ Everyone closes their eyes when they feel comfortable and thinks about the safest place they can imagine.
- ⊗ Maybe it needs a journey to get there?
- ⊗ Think about what kind of land leads to the safe place. Open fields? A mysterious forest? A special garden? Some other landscape?
- ⊗ Imagine you are making a journey to your special place, and when you get there relax quietly.
- ⊗ Slowly make the journey home and take time to stretch and open your eyes.

Sharing Allow time to surface from the relaxation; stretch and yawn.

Closure Create a calm picture in the workbooks; relax with fleeces.

Body Learning

45 Creative Visualisation 2

✓ Children ✓ Teenagers

Aims To develop an imaginative approach to distractions and worries.

Materials Large whiteboard & coloured markers, drums, blank paper & folders, workbooks, crayons & coloured pens, mats, fleeces.

Warm-Up Invite everyone into the circle and allow time for feedback and questions. Explain the aim of the session, which is to encourage everyone to develop their imagination in order to deal with distractions and worries.

Physical warm-up General shake-out, then everyone lies on the floor, stretches and yawns several times.

Activities Everyone lies on their mats, with a fleece close by, while you lead them on an imaginary journey:

- ✪ Each person lies comfortably on their back or side. Encourage everyone to breathe deeply, in through the nose and out through the mouth.
- ✪ Describe the journey, leaving a garden, crossing a field towards a wood (linger on detail, such as the colours, sounds and smells encountered).
- ✪ At the edge of the wood there stands the Worry Tree; lots of little scrolls are tied to the tree with red ribbon.
- ✪ Everyone imagines that they are writing down one of their worries on a small piece of paper, rolling it up with red ribbon, and then tying it to the tree.
- ✪ Slowly make the journey back to the garden again; very slowly open your eyes and sit up.

Sharing Allow time to surface from the relaxation: stretch and yawn.

Closure Draw the tree in the workbooks; relax with fleeces.

Body Learning

46 Letting Go 1

 Children ✓ Teenagers

> **Aims** To give participants autonomy to focus their energy and decrease their own anxiety.

> **Materials** Large whiteboard & coloured markers, drums, blank paper & folders, workbooks, crayons & coloured pens, mats, fleeces; music player, Reiki relaxation music, or similar.

Warm-Up Invite everyone into the circle and allow time for feedback and questions. Explain the aim of the session, which is to acknowledge that people get tense through worries and that learning to relax their bodies can help to change them.

Physical warm-up 'Shake-out' and play 'chase' with a partner around the room.

Activities Play the music softly and have everyone lie on their mat with a fleece nearby:

- ✪ Stretch the legs and arms and have a big, noisy yawn; close the eyes if possible.
- ✪ Clench the right foot and let it go, then repeat; stretch the right leg and it let go, then repeat.
- ✪ Repeat, clenching and releasing left foot and leg twice.
- ✪ Tense the tummy muscles and let go, repeat; tense the chest muscles and let go, repeat.
- ✪ Clench the right hand and let go, repeat; stretch the right arm and let go, repeat.
- ✪ Repeat, clenching and releasing the left hand and arm twice.
- ✪ Slowly move the head from side to side to relax the neck muscles.
- ✪ Screw the face up and relax, twice.
- ✪ Frown hard and then raise eyebrows up as high as possible; repeat.
- ✪ Take some deep breaths and slowly turn up the Reiki music for five minutes' relaxation.

> **Sharing** Very slowly stretch, open the eyes and sit up. Allow recovery time.

> **Closure** Draw any growing plant in the workbooks; relax with fleeces.

47 Letting Go 2

✓ Children ✓ Teenagers

Aims To refocus on the body and change anxiety patterns.

Materials Large whiteboard & coloured markers, drums, blank paper & folders, workbooks, crayons & coloured pens, mats, fleeces; soft ball, music player, recordings of whale and dolphin sounds.

Warm-Up Invite everyone into the circle and allow time for feedback and questions. Explain the aims of the session, which are to find ways to relax and focus on the 'now'!

Physical warm-up Football or 'catch' with a soft ball.

Activities Play the whale and dolphin calls quietly and explain the sounds to the group. Have everyone lie on their mat with a fleece nearby:

- ❸ Invite everyone to have a stretch and yawn, closing their eyes if comfortable.
- ❸ Slowly bring up the whale sounds and music.
- ❸ Allow the music to play for five minutes (or less if concentration is difficult).
- ❸ Remind people to breathe deeply and to imagine the whales and dolphins slowly swimming in the ocean.
- ❸ Slowly fade the music down.

Sharing Everyone takes time to stretch, opens their eyes and sits up; take time to surface and share thoughts when ready.

Closure Draw a whale or a dolphin in the workbooks; relax with fleeces.

Body Learning

48 Switching Off 1

 ✓ Children ◯ Teenagers

Aims To address issues of anxiety and replace these with relaxing images.

Materials Large whiteboard & coloured markers, drums, blank paper & folders, workbooks, crayons & coloured pens, mats, fleeces.

Warm-Up Invite everyone into the circle and allow time for feedback and questions. Explain the aim of the session, which is to learn how to focus on positive images instead of negative ones, to help concentration.

Physical warm-up Skip in a circle; gallop in a circle, first to the right then to the left.

Activities Make coloured pens, crayons and paper available and ask everyone to relax on a mat with their fleece nearby:

- ✪ Everyone curls up in a comfortable position, closing their eyes if possible.
- ✪ Picture yourself in a garden where there are lots of things to play on: swings, slides, climbing frames, and so on.
- ✪ Play on your favourite apparatus with other children in the group.
- ✪ Hold hands with a partner and spin around and around … then fall over.
- ✪ See yourself lying on the grass looking up at a big blue sky.

Sharing Slowly stretch and open the eyes; look around the group and see the people who were in your garden.

Closure Draw something from the garden in the workbooks; relax with fleeces.

 ⓟ This page may be photocopied for instructional use only. *101 Activities for Increasing Focus & Motivation* © Sue Jennings 2015

Body Learning

49 Switching Off 2

○ Children ☑ Teenagers

Aims To change body patterns in order to develop greater focus.

Materials Large whiteboard & coloured markers, drums, blank paper & folders, workbooks, crayons & coloured pens, mats, fleeces; soft ball.

Warm-Up Invite everyone into the circle and allow time for feedback and questions. Explain the aim of the session, which is to support participants in finding new ways to focus through picturing themselves succeeding.

Physical warm-up The group chooses any game to play together using the soft ball.

Activities Everyone relaxes on a mat with fleeces nearby:

- ✪ Invite everyone to stretch and yawn and to close their eyes if comfortable.
- ✪ Curl up in a comfy position.
- ✪ Picture in your mind a favourite sport that you are competing in at the Olympics. (Maybe it is a sport you have never played!)
- ✪ You have your kit, you do your warm-up, and take your place, ready to start.
- ✪ You start! Everyone is cheering; there you are, finishing with the medallists!

Body Learning

Sharing Slowly stretch, open the eyes and sit up. Take time to recover.

Closure Draw a picture of your sport in the workbooks; relax with fleeces.

50 Death by Winking

 Children ✓ Teenagers

Aims Developing a game to encourage focus and attention.

Materials Large whiteboard & coloured markers, drums, blank paper & folders, workbooks, crayons & coloured pens, mats, fleeces.

Warm-Up Invite everyone into the circle and allow time for feedback and questions. Explain the aim of the session, which is to learn a game that can help focus attention.

Physical warm-up Everyone stands in a circle and looks around the group at everyone else, smiles and stretches all the muscles in their faces.

Activities With everyone still standing in the circle, explain the game:

- One person, the detective, goes out of the room.
- Everyone closes their eyes while the group leader walks around the circle and touches several people on the shoulder (they will be the 'killers').
- The detective comes back into the room and stands in centre of circle.
- The 'killers' now have to wink at someone in the group, without anyone noticing except the person being winked at – and those people fall down 'dead'.
- The detective has to find the 'killers' by seeing them wink. People keep being 'winked to death' until all the 'killers' are caught.

Sharing The group discusses the game and how much concentration was needed in the different roles.

Closure Draw a face winking the workbooks; relax with fleeces.

Body Learning

Part Six
Understanding Feelings

Children and teenagers who have difficulty in maintaining a focus or in being motivated to learn are often struggling to manage their feelings. They may be distracted by overwhelming feelings that they do not understand, or they may be preoccupied with violent or cruel experiences. Children who have been abused have great difficulty in make sense of their world; teenagers who have been abandoned do not know how to trust others and show affection. We learn how to express our feelings appropriately by observing a role model, but if there is no appropriate role model in a young person's life this learning may not take place.

Most children and teenagers struggle to express their feelings, so the use of themed cards or images will capture the imagination, often unexpectedly, and allow group members to express their feelings in a less direct way. Images in the card packs can suddenly trigger an individual to make a mental connection that helps make sense of their world.

It is most important that the individual's feelings are validated. Whether or not the feelings make any sense to others, these feelings still need to be acknowledged. For some individuals this may be the first time they have received any acknowledgement of how they feel. As stated in the previous section, the body is central to our expression of emotion, and it may be that feelings are buried so deeply that it takes time for them to emerge.

Activities

51 How's My World? 1

52 How's My World 2

53 How's My World? 3

54 How's My World? 4

55 Family Life 1

56 Family Life 2

57 Family Life 3

58 Family Life Role Plays 1

59 Family Life Role Plays 2

60 Family Life Cartoons

Resources

⊗ Your own collection of images depicting feelings and emotions (from magazines or online resources)

⊗ Your own collection of images of family life (from magazines or online resources)

Alternatively:

⊗ Card sets such as 'How's My World?' (Rogerson, 2014).

51 How's My World?

✓ Children ✓ Teenagers

Aims Through images depicting feelings and emotions, participants gain insight into changes they would like to make in their own lives.

Materials Large whiteboard & coloured markers, drums, blank paper & folders, workbooks, crayons & coloured pens, mats, fleeces; feelings and emotions pictures or cards, e.g. 'How's My World?' card set.

Warm-Up Invite everyone into the circle and allow time for feedback and questions. Explain the aims of the session, which are to encourage everyone to connect with feelings that are perhaps bottled up inside and to seek ways to transform them.

Physical warm-up The group chooses a warm-up from Resources, Warm-Up Games.

Activities Prepare the feelings and emotions images and give everyone paper, coloured pens or crayons:

- ✪ Pass the pictures or cards around, allowing time for everyone to look.
- ✪ Allow group members to choose an image that they feel a connection with.
- ✪ Talk with a partner about the connection.
- ✪ Acknowledge the bottled-up feelings expressed in the picture.
- ✪ Make suggestions to each other of possible ways to transform these feelings.

Sharing Discuss the images in the group and allow time for commenting on other pictures.

Closure Draw a positive image from the session in the workbooks; relax with fleeces.

Ⓟ This page may be photocopied for instructional use only. *101 Activities for Increasing Focus & Motivation* © Sue Jennings 2015

Understanding Feelings

52 How's My World? 2

☑ Children ☑ Teenagers

Understanding Feelings

Aims	To encourage group members to acknowledge any feelings that may be troubling them.

Materials	Large whiteboard & coloured markers, drums, blank paper & folders, workbooks, crayons & coloured pens, mats, fleeces; feelings and emotions pictures or cards, e.g. 'How's My World?' card set.

Warm-Up   Invite everyone into the circle and allow time for feedback and questions. Explain the aim of the session, which is to acknowledge feelings that get in the way of concentration.

Physical warm-up   Group members choose their own warm-up from Resources, Warm-Up Games.

Activities   Prepare the feelings and emotions images and give everyone coloured pens or crayons and paper:

- ✪ Spread the pictures or cards out in a circle.
- ✪ Everyone takes time to look at them.
- ✪ Each person chooses one image (several people can choose the same one) and copies the picture in the centre of their piece of paper.
- ✪ Think of what might surround this image and draw ideas for the whole landscape.
- ✪ Reflect on the possible dangers in the landscape and what can be done about them.

Sharing	Place all the pictures on the floor and see if the landscapes join up; share a danger and a possible solution to this.

Closure	Draw or write about something 'protective' in the workbooks; relax with fleeces.

 ℗ This page may be photocopied for instructional use only. *101 Activities for Increasing Focus & Motivation* © Sue Jennings 2015

53 How's My World? 3

☑ Children ☑ Teenagers

Aims Stimulating the imagination to come up with alternative life choices.

Materials Large whiteboard & coloured markers, drums, blank paper & folders, workbooks, crayons & coloured pens, mats, fleeces; feelings and emotions pictures or cards, e.g. 'How's My World?' card set.

Warm-Up Invite everyone into the circle and allow time for feedback and questions. Explain the aim of the session, which is to encourage everyone to think of positive alternatives in their lives, using the images or cards as prompts.

Physical warm-up Group members choose their own warm-up from Resources, Warm-Up Games.

Activities Prepare the feelings and emotions images and give everyone coloured pens or crayons and paper:

- ❂ Spread the pictures or cards out on the floor in a circle.
- ❂ Invite everyone to choose an image that could represent a more positive future.
- ❂ Copy the image onto blank paper.
- ❂ Colour the picture and add anything else that could be in the future.
- ❂ What is the most important thing that needs to change to make this image more real in your life?

Sharing Talk about future choices in the whole group.

Closure Draw or write down a positive future image in the workbooks; relax with fleeces.

Understanding Feelings

54 How's My World? 4

☑ Children ☑ Teenagers

Understanding Feelings

> **Aims** To encourage risk-taking and imaginative solutions.

> **Materials** Large whiteboard & coloured markers, drums, blank paper & folders, workbooks, crayons & coloured pens, mats, fleeces; feelings and emotions pictures or cards, e.g. 'How's My World?' card set.

Warm-Up Invite everyone into the circle and allow time for feedback and questions. Explain the aim of the session, which is to play with ideas.

Physical warm-up Group members choose their own warm-up from Resources, Warm-Up Games.

Activities Prepare the feelings and emotions images and give everyone coloured pens or crayons and paper:

- ✪ Spread the pictures or cards face down in a circle.
- ✪ Invite pairs to choose an image and look at it.
- ✪ Think of a scene that the image suggests.
- ✪ In small groups, dramatise the scene, thinking about causes and consequences.
- ✪ Share the scenes with each other.

> **Sharing** Give feedback to each other about scenes and look at the original pictures.

> **Closure** Draw or write the title of a new play in the workbooks; relax with fleeces.

 ℗ This page may be photocopied for instructional use only. *101 Activities for Increasing Focus & Motivation* © Sue Jennings 2015

55 Family Life 1

☑ Children ☑ Teenagers

Aims To give opportunities for group members to safely explore family themes in order to improve focus and motivation.

Materials Large whiteboard & coloured markers, drums, blank paper & folders, workbooks, crayons & coloured pens, mats, fleeces; pictures or cards showing family scenes with both positive and negative emotions.

Warm-Up Invite everyone into the circle and allow time for feedback and questions. Explain the aim of the session, which is to explore family themes that may distract participants from their tasks.

Physical warm-up Group members choose one or more warm-ups from Resources, Warm-Up Games.

Activities Use the images of family life as prompts:

- ✪ Spread the pictures or cards in a circle for everyone to look at.
- ✪ Everyone chooses one card and then forms into groups of three.
- ✪ Discuss the cards in groups and choose one card from the three to use to create a family scene.
- ✪ Experiment with playing the different roles.
- ✪ Practise one scene to share with the group.

Sharing Show the scenes to the whole group and give each other feedback.

Closure Draw a stick-person family scene in the workbooks; relax with fleeces.

Understanding Feelings

56 Family Life 2

 Children ✓ Teenagers

Aims To encourage insight into family dynamics through the use of simple dramatic symbols, and to create opportunities for change.

Materials Large whiteboard & coloured markers, drums, blank paper & folders, workbooks, crayons & coloured pens, mats, fleeces; pictures or cards showing family scenes with both positive and negative emotions.

Warm-Up Invite everyone into the circle and allow time for feedback and questions. Explain the aims of the session, which are to explore and understand what goes on in families.

Physical warm-up Group members choose one or more warm-ups from Resources, Warm-Up Games.

Activities Use the images of family life as prompts:

- ⊗ Spread the pictures or cards out in a circle.
- ⊗ In groups of four, choose one card and discuss what might have lead to the scene and its consequences.
- ⊗ Create three body sculpts (see Introduction, How to Structure a Session: Explanation of core techniques). These should show the beginning, middle and end of the scene.
- ⊗ Share the sculpts in whole group.
- ⊗ Give feedback within the groups of four.

Sharing Share opinions about the different sculpts with the whole group.

Closure Draw a stick-person family scene in the workbooks; relax with fleeces.

57 Family Life 3

 Children ☑ Teenagers

> **Aims** To facilitate more advanced insight into family dynamics through the use of simple dramatic symbols.

> **Materials** Large whiteboard & coloured markers, drums, blank paper & folders, workbooks, crayons & coloured pens, mats, fleeces; pictures or cards showing family scenes with both positive and negative emotions.

Warm-Up Invite everyone into the circle and allow time for feedback and questions. Explain the aim of the session, which is to expand understanding of family life.

Physical warm-up Group members choose one or more warm-ups from Resources, Warm-Up Games.

Activities Use the images of family life as prompts:

- ✪ Spread the pictures or cards out, face down, in the circle.
- ✪ Everyone chooses a card.
- ✪ Each person mimes the image on their card to the group using gestures only.
- ✪ The group tries to guess what the card represents.
- ✪ Repeat, with groups of three choosing one card to mime between them.

> **Sharing** Discuss how difficult it is to communicate without using words.

> **Closure** Draw a stick-person family scene in the workbooks; relax with fleeces.

Understanding Feelings

58 Family Life Role Plays 1

 Children ✓ Teenagers

Aims To use role play to show how the lives of families we see in the media can distract us.

Materials Large whiteboard & coloured markers, drums, blank paper & folders, workbooks, crayons & coloured pens, mats, fleeces.

Warm-Up Invite everyone into the circle and allow time for feedback and questions. Explain the aim of the session, which is to explore the images of life in famous families that the media bring into our homes and how we might compare our own lives to these.

Physical warm-up Group members choose one or warm-ups from Resources, Warm-Up Games.

Activities Invite discussion about well-known families that people might read about in newspapers or see on TV:

- ⊗ Are these families different from our own, everyday, families?
- ⊗ Do famous people have to face particular difficulties?
- ⊗ Form groups of three, and choose a situation people have heard about to explore through sculpting.
- ⊗ How does it feel to role-play a famous person?
- ⊗ Add words to the sculpt and show the scene to whole group.

Sharing Discuss the themes and see if they have changed after the role play.

Closure Draw or write a famous, respected name in the workbooks; relax with fleeces.

Understanding Feelings

Family Life Role Plays 2

✓ Children ✓ Teenagers

Aims To make use of scenes from TV soaps and other programmes to encourage insight into family life.

Materials Large whiteboard & coloured markers, drums, blank paper & folders, workbooks, crayons & coloured pens, mats, fleeces; dressing-up clothes, cloth and other dramatic props.

Warm-Up Invite everyone into the circle and allow time for feedback and questions. Explain the aims of the session, which are to identify and understand scenes that dramatise family dynamics.

Physical warm-up Group members choose their favourite warm-up from Resources, Warm-Up Games.

Activities Suggest that the group discuss different TV soaps, or any other programme that depicts family life (family game shows, for example):

- ✪ In groups of three, choose one soap/programme and a typical scene.
- ✪ Discuss the scene and how to enact it.
- ✪ Make use of cloths, props.
- ✪ Play the scene to the other group members.
- ✪ Encourage comment and feedback.

Sharing Discuss what can be understood about how families interact through watching TV families.

Closure Draw a stick-person family in the workbooks; relax with fleeces.

Understanding Feelings

60 Family Life Cartoons

 Children ☑ Teenagers

Aims To understand more about families through the use of cartoons.

Materials Large whiteboard & coloured markers, drums, blank paper & folders, workbooks, crayons & coloured pens, mats, fleeces.

Warm-Up Invite everyone into the circle and allow time for feedback and questions. Explain the aim of the session, which is to understand more about how families function through humour.

Physical warm-up Group members choose their favourite warm-up from Resources, Warm-Up Games.

Activities Each person has paper, coloured pens and pencils:

- ✪ Invite everyone to divide their paper into four squares.
- ✪ Think about a scene that might take place in a family.
- ✪ Draw it as a funny cartoon story across the four squares, don't worry about drawing skills, stick people are fine.
- ✪ Write dialogue in speech balloons coming out of the characters' mouths.
- ✪ Give your cartoon a title.

Sharing Show the cartoons to whole group and compare similarities.

Closure Draw a favourite cartoon in the workbooks; relax with fleeces.

Understanding Feelings

Part Seven
Drumming a New Rhythm

As discussed earlier, rhythmic play is essential to early human development and this method aims to emphasise rhythmic ways of moving and greater awareness of heartbeats. In this section the possibilities of developing rhythmic work are expanded, with the idea of encouraging children and teenagers to become 're-rhythmed' in order to relax, calm and refocus. Kelly Hunter (2014) has established a rhythmic approach to working with young people on the autistic spectrum, through use of Shakespeare's speeches. It is fascinating to note that the rhythm of these speeches often follows the pattern of the human heartbeat.

Working with a variety of rhythmic exercises and drums, rhythm can be re-established for both individuals and groups. Fun can be had with drums or clapping, and group members can take it in turn to lead with a rhythm. Rhythm is also linked to breathing, and heartbeats can be slowed down by the use of deep breathing. Being able to breathe deeply helps group members to gain control over their own breathing patterns and to let go of tensions and stress.

Rhythmic warm-ups (in which group members walk or run in the same rhythm), clapping games and spinning, marching and skipping, all encourage the establishment of rhythm, both internal and external.

Activities

61 Heartbeats

62 The Heart Tree 1

63 The Heart Tree 2

64 Breathing in Rhythms 1

65 Breathing in Rhythms 2

66 Rhythmic Speech 1

67 Rhythmic Speech 2

68 Rhythmic Speech 3

69 Playing with Rhythmic Scenes 1

70 Playing with Rhythmic Scenes 2

Worksheet

13 The Heart Tree

61 Heartbeats

 ✓ Children ✓ Teenagers

> **Aims** To connect group members with the rhythm of their bodies and increase awareness.

> **Materials** Large whiteboard & coloured markers, drums, blank paper & folders, workbooks, crayons & coloured pens, mats, fleeces; stethoscope.

Warm-Up Invite everyone into the circle and allow time for feedback and questions. Explain the aim of the session, which is to explore the primary rhythms that everyone hears from birth.

Physical warm-up Sit in a circle and pass a clap around the circle, then pass it in both directions, then pass a double clap in one direction, then a double clap in both directions.

Activities Encourage group members to sit and breathe deeply:

- ✪ Invite them to find their own heartbeat and be aware of its rhythm.
- ✪ Take it in turns to listen to your own heart beating.
- ✪ Take it in turns to listen to a partner's heart.
- ✪ Compare beats and clap your own heartbeat.
- ✪ Combine different heartbeats in the group with clapping or clicking fingers.

> **Sharing** Share your knowledge base about the heart and why a healthy beat is important.

> **Closure** Draw a heart in the workbooks and colour it; relax with fleeces.

Drumming a New Rhythm

62 The Heart Tree 1

 ✓ Children ○ Teenagers

Drumming a New Rhythm

Aims To encourage the symbol of the heart as a motif representing positive feelings and motivation.

Materials Large whiteboard & coloured markers, drums, blank paper & folders, workbooks, crayons & coloured pens, mats, fleeces; Worksheet 13 'The Heart Tree'.

Warm-Up Invite everyone into the circle and allow time for feedback and questions. Explain the aim of the session, which is to explore the symbol of the heart and its ability to help us focus on positive feelings.

Physical warm-up Play the circle game 'I sent a letter to my love'.

Activities Each person has coloured pens or crayons and Worksheet 13, 'The Heart Tree':

- ⊗ Think about the Heart Tree.
- ⊗ Allow positive feelings to be expressed.
- ⊗ Colour all the hearts and the tree.
- ⊗ Write some names in hearts if wished.
- ⊗ Colour in the landscape.

Sharing Show your picture to a partner and decide on something kind to do for someone else.

Closure Draw a heart on a leaf in the workbooks; relax with fleeces.

63 The Heart Tree 2

◯ Children ☑ Teenagers

Aims To allow 'softer feelings' to come through and to learn to express emotional needs.

Materials Large whiteboard & coloured markers, drums, blank paper & folders, workbooks, crayons & coloured pens, mats, fleeces; Worksheet 13 'The Heart Tree'.

Warm-Up Invite everyone into the circle and allow time for feedback and questions. Explain the aim of the session, which is to encourage the expression of positive feelings.

Physical warm-up Make up a game in which everyone builds up a joint clap; then one person changes it and everyone follows the new clap; keep the claps going without breaking the sequence.

Activities Each person has coloured pens or crayons and Worksheet 13, 'The Heart Tree':

- ✪ Discuss pictures of hearts in the media, on t-shirts, athletes' gestures of holding a clenched fist to their hearts when winning or scoring.
- ✪ Note that the motif of the heart is often used instead of the word 'love'.
- ✪ Colour the Heart Tree and the hearts.
- ✪ Write the names of people or favourite activities inside the hearts if wished.
- ✪ Colour the landscape around the tree.

Sharing Show your picture to a partner and talk about choices; decide on something kind to do for someone else.

Closure Draw a heart person in the workbooks; relax with fleeces.

Ⓟ This page may be photocopied for instructional use only. *101 Activities for Increasing Focus & Motivation* © Sue Jennings 2015

Drumming a New Rhythm

64 Breathing in Rhythms 1

☑ Children ◯ Teenagers

Aims To support children in changing their rhythmic patterns and finding new rhythms that are stimulating.

Materials Large whiteboard & coloured markers, drums, blank paper & folders, workbooks, crayons & coloured pens, mats, fleeces.

Warm-Up Invite everyone into the circle and allow time for feedback and questions. Explain the aim of the session, which is to develop new rhythms through drumming and chanting.

Physical warm-up Some of the group have drums and play while the others move; swap roles.

Activities Everyone has a partner and each couple (if possible) shares one stout drum. Together they experiment with different ways of playing/performing:

- ✪ One person could play while the other moves; change roles.
- ✪ Two people beat one drum and try to coordinate their rhythm.
- ✪ Create a chant to go with the drumbeat.
- ✪ Start very quietly and build up to loud; then gradually play more quietly again.
- ✪ Play and chant at a sound level that feels right.

Sharing Show the drumming and chanting sequences to the whole group and gradually create a continuous piece.

Closure Draw a drum in the workbooks; relax with fleeces.

65 Breathing in Rhythms 2

◯ Children   ✓ Teenagers

> **Aims** To support group members in experimenting with varying rhythms and discovering new patterns.

> **Materials** Large whiteboard & coloured markers, drums, blank paper & folders, workbooks, crayons & coloured pens, mats, fleeces.

Warm-Up Invite everyone into the circle and allow time for feedback and questions. Explain the aim of the session, which is to find new rhythms through drumming and chanting.

Physical warm-up Some people play drums for the others to move; swap around.

Activities Everyone has a partner and each couple (if possible) shares one stout drum:

- ✪ Experiment with taking it in turns to play drum rhythms.
- ✪ Add chanting with simple sounds.
- ✪ Offer the rhythm and chant for other groups to dance to.
- ✪ Explore dance shapes through improvisation.
- ✪ Put together a rhythm, chant and dance as an integrated piece.

> **Sharing** Show the pieces to the group and learn how to be an attentive audience.

> **Closure** Draw and colour a footprint in the workbooks; relax with fleeces.

Drumming a New Rhythm

66 Rhythmic Speech 1

✓ Children ✓ Teenagers

Aims To develop poetry and rhythmic speech as extensions of the heartbeat so that they become 'natural' rhythms.

Materials Large whiteboard & coloured markers, drums, blank paper & folders, workbooks, crayons & coloured pens, mats, fleeces.

Warm-Up Invite everyone into the circle and allow time for feedback and questions. Explain the aim of the session, which is to develop rhythms in speech that are helpful to our understanding and memory.

Physical warm-up Practise different ways of running that emphasise different beats.

Activities Write on the whiteboard:

> I know a bank where the wild thyme blows,
> Where oxlips and the nodding violet grows,
>
> *A Midsummer Night's Dream*, 2:i

- ✪ Encourage the group to say the quotation all together and allow the natural rhythm to emerge. (They will find it much easier to remember once they use the rhythm!)
- ✪ Walk around the room saying the phrase loud, soft, and under the breath.
- ✪ In twos, one person says the first line and their partner replies with the second; change over.
- ✪ Then one person says their line and the other begins before they have finished, so that the two lines overlap.

Sharing Discuss the exercise in the whole group and comment on whether or not it became easier.

Closure Draw and colour a violet or oxlip in the workbooks; relax with fleeces.

67 Rhythmic Speech 2

☑ Children   ☑ Teenagers

> **Aims**   To encourage rhythmic speech as a way of building confidence and self-assurance.

> **Materials**   Large whiteboard & coloured markers, drums, blank paper & folders, workbooks, crayons & coloured pens, mats, fleeces.

Warm-Up   Invite everyone into the circle and allow time for feedback and questions. Explain the aim of the session, which is to encourage rhythmic speech as a means to increase confidence.

Physical warm-up   Any physical movement that involves rhythm, such as skipping, hopping, marching, and so on.

Activities   Write on the board:

> If we shadows have offended,
> Think but this and all is mended –
>
> *A Midsummer Night's Dream*, 5:i

- ✪ Check everyone understands the meaning of the quote.
- ✪ Practise saying the two phrases until they flow.
- ✪ Clap the beat of the words as they are said.
- ✪ Move around the room saying the phrases alone, then with a partner, then as an echo to the partner.

> **Sharing**   Discuss the meaning of the phrase in the whole group, especially the word 'shadows'.

> **Closure**   Draw a shadow picture in the workbooks; relax with fleeces.

Drumming a New Rhythm

68 Rhythmic Speech 3

 Children ✓ Teenagers

Aims To create new patterns of movement and speech that encourage changes in motivational attitudes.

Materials Large whiteboard & coloured markers, drums, blank paper & folders, workbooks, crayons & coloured pens, mats, fleeces.

Warm-Up Invite everyone into the circle and allow time for feedback and questions. Explain the aims of the session, which are to change rhythms and patterns and to inspire creative movement and speech.

Physical warm-up Move around the room and say, 'My mistress with a monster is in love', in several different ways.

Activities The following ideas can be developed in a 'larger than life' fashion. Explain that the quotation they have just used is from *A Midsummer Night's Dream* and that it is a comment by Puck, a servant of the King of the Fairies. One of the other characters has had a donkey's head magically placed on his shoulders – and now the Queen of the Fairies has fallen in love with him!

- ✪ With a partner, say the phrase to each other in a whisper, then very loudly, with great exaggeration.
- ✪ Experiment with emphasising different words in the phrase.
- ✪ One person takes on the role of Puck and the other takes on the role of Oberon, King of the Fairies. Puck says the line and Oberon responds.
- ✪ Change roles and practise the interaction until it becomes 'right'.

Sharing Discuss in the whole group how it feels for one person to make someone else looks silly; suggest that it is OK for this to happen in a play but not in everyday life.

Closure Draw and colour the donkey's head in the workbooks; relax with fleeces.

Drumming a New Rhythm

69 Playing with Rhythmic Scenes 1

 Children ✓ Teenagers

Aims To integrate the previous learning of rhythm and movement in order to build security through rhythm.

Materials Large whiteboard & coloured markers, drums, blank paper & folders, workbooks, crayons & coloured pens, mats, fleeces; stapler, scissors, several pieces of card and a baseball cap for each person.

Warm-Up Invite everyone into the circle and allow time for feedback and questions. Explain the aims of the session, which are to dramatise scenes and to build confidence.

Physical warm-up Walk as a king, a mischievous 'sprite' (Puck), a heavy workman, a flying creature.

Activities Each person has scissors, several pieces of card, coloured pens or crayons and a baseball cap; staplers may be shared:

- ✪ In groups of three, cut out ears for the donkey, small wings for Puck and a crown for King Oberon.
- ✪ Fix or stick them onto each of the baseball caps to create three props.
- ✪ Create scenes in which Puck puts the 'donkey's head' on a workman (Bottom).
- ✪ Then a scene in which Oberon is told what has happened.
- ✪ Play with the roles and take turns with different characters.

Sharing Compare how it felt to play the different roles.

Closure Draw wings in the workbooks; relax with fleeces.

Drumming a New Rhythm

70 Playing with Rhythmic Scenes 2

 Children ☑ Teenagers

Aims To continue developing scenes and characters in order to build confidence in movement and speech.

Materials Large whiteboard & coloured markers, drums, blank paper & folders, workbooks, crayons & coloured pens, mats, fleeces; card, scissors and baseball cap for each person, stapler, large pieces of cloth in bright colours. Story Sheet 1 'A Midsummer Night's Dream'.

Warm-Up Invite everyone into the circle and allow time for feedback and questions. Explain the aim of the session, which is to continue working with the scenes and characters of the previous session.

Physical warm-up Walk proudly, mischievously, slowly and heavily, then lightly, with your feet only briefly touching the ground.

Activities Continue with the dramatisation started in Activity 69:

- ⊗ In groups of three, discuss elaborating the scenes between Oberon, Puck and Bottom. For example, show Bottom at his job weaving cloth in the market, and Puck and Oberon planning the trick to play on Titania.

- ⊗ Practice some of the scenes using body sculpting – each person 'freezing' a movement, without using words.

- ⊗ Create a sequence of body sculpts of the characters, and then a final scene in which the donkey's head is placed on Bottom and Puck reports to Oberon.

- ⊗ Share the scenes with the whole group.

Sharing Read the abbreviated story of the entire play in the Resources section (Story Sheet 1 'A Midsummer Night's Dream'), and notice how the scenes in which Bottom wears the donkey's head fit into the whole.

Closure Draw a crown in the workbooks; relax with fleeces.

Part Eight
Activities I Enjoy: Sports & Games

Sports and games can present a series of dilemmas for teachers and facilitators. Very often it is only the very best young people who are picked for the team, because school or club sport is usually highly competitive. The message is that if you are not a first-rate athlete, you might as well not bother! Since many schools no longer have playing fields, it can be very difficult in any case to ensure sporting opportunities for all those who would like to participate.

I remember my personal conflicts when I went to a school with a very sporty headmistress. My father did not think hockey was 'ladylike' – and certainly not for a budding dancer! Correspondence went back and forth, and meanwhile I had to walk around and around the playing field, the butt of humour for pupils and staff alike. I had no sporting confidence thereafter and certainly no motivation!

Gentle sporting routines that start as games and slowly build up to greater skills, can be helpful for building confidence. Non-focussed children are often uncoordinated and need a lot of physical activity (and rhythmic work) that will build up their skills – and also their interest. Children and teenagers need to be engaged with the physical process, but it may feel scary or impossible, or as if they have begun something that will be yet another failure. The attention being paid to rhythm and relaxation in earlier sections all provide a firm foundation to encourage physical involvement.

Activities

71 Activities I Enjoy: Sports 1

72 Activities I Enjoy: Sports 2

73 Activities I Enjoy: Sports & Games 1

74 Activities I Enjoy: Sports & Games 2

75 Activities I Enjoy: Sports & Games 3

76 An Activity I Would Like: Games 1

77 An Activity I Would Like: Games 2

78 An Activity I Would Like: Games 3

79 An Activity I Would Like: Games 4

80 An Activity I Would Like: Board Game

Worksheets

14 Activities I Enjoy: Sport

15 Sports & Games: Tug of Rope

16 Sports & Games: Swinging & Running

17 Sports & Games: Football & Rugby

18 Activities I Enjoy: Collections

71 Activities I Enjoy: Sports 1

☑ Children ☑ Teenagers

Aims To encourage participants to focus on activities they enjoy and to develop positive experiences.

Materials Large whiteboard & coloured markers, drums, blank paper & folders, workbooks, crayons & coloured pens, mats, fleeces; large soft ball, magazines with varied sporting pictures, scissors, glue.

Warm-Up Invite everyone into the circle and allow time for feedback and questions. Explain the aims of the session, which are to find enjoyable activities and perhaps discover new ones.

Physical warm-up Throw the soft ball to each other, calling out your name as you throw; start again, but this time call out the name of the catcher.

Activities Everyone has blank paper or card, coloured pens or crayons, sports magazines, scissors and glue:

- ✪ Everyone chooses pictures of sports they like to play or to watch.
- ✪ Cut out the favourites and glue them together as a collage.
- ✪ Use coloured pens to fill in any gaps between the pictures.
- ✪ Work out a star-rating system for the pictures that are liked best.

Sharing In pairs, look at your collages and discuss the similarities and differences.

Closure Draw one favourite sport in the workbooks; relax with fleeces.

---

72 Activities I Enjoy: Sports 2

 ✓ Children ✓ Teenagers

Aims To encourage participants to focus on activities they enjoy and to develop positive experiences.

Materials Large whiteboard & coloured markers, drums, blank paper & folders, workbooks, crayons & coloured pens, mats, fleeces; sporting magazines, scissors, glue, Worksheet 14 'Activities I Enjoy: Sport'.

Warm-Up Invite everyone into the circle and allow time for feedback and questions. Explain the aim of the session, which is to continue to find enjoyable activities.

Physical warm-up Call out different sports and everyone has to mime doing that sport, no words can be used, only bodies: tennis, football, ice hockey, and so on.

Activities Each person has blank paper or card, coloured pens or crayons, sports magazines, scissors and glue, as well as Worksheet 14, 'Activities I Enjoy: Sport':

- ⊗ Everyone has a choice of drawing or cutting out pictures from sports magazines or doing a combination of both.
- ⊗ Invite everyone to use the circle on the worksheet to create their own circle picture of their favourite sports.
- ⊗ Include sports that are enjoyable to watch as well as those people like to play.
- ⊗ Colour the gaps between pictures, and write four words to describe how you feel about your favourite sports activities.

Sharing In small groups, compare your circle pictures, their similarities and differences.

Closure Write or draw one sport you would like to play in the workbooks; relax with fleeces.

73 Activities I Enjoy: Sports & Games 1

 ✓ Children   ✓ Teenagers

> **Aims** To encourage participation in collaborative sports and games, rather than just competitive activities.

> **Materials** Large whiteboard & coloured markers, drums, blank paper & folders, workbooks, crayons & coloured pens, mats, fleeces; large soft ball or a strong balloon.

Warm-Up Invite everyone into the circle and allow time for feedback and questions. Explain the aims of the session, which are to develop new sports skills and experience in playing collaborative games.

Physical warm-up Two people hold hands and then another pair stand behind them, holding hands and holding the first couple by their waists with their free hands. Keep adding another pair, until the whole group is holding each other by the waist and trying not to overbalance.

Activities Using a large soft ball or a strong balloon:

- ✪ Everyone tries to keep it in the air for as long as possible.
- ✪ Two teams try to keep it going back and forth for as long as possible.
- ✪ Pass the ball or balloon from person to person using both knees.
- ✪ Balance it on the hand and pass it to the next person.

> **Sharing** Group discussion of how it felt to collaborate, rather than to compete.

> **Closure** Draw a balloon in your favourite colour in the workbooks; relax with fleeces.

Activities I Enjoy: Sports & Games

74 Activities I Enjoy: Sports & Games 2

 Children ✓ Teenagers

Aims To reinforce collaboration in activities as a means to increasing motivation.

Materials Large whiteboard & coloured markers, drums, blank paper & folders, workbooks, crayons & coloured pens, mats, fleeces; Worksheet 15 'Sports & Games: Tug of Rope'.

Warm-Up Invite everyone into the circle and allow time for feedback and questions. Explain the aim of the session, which is to explore different team sports that need collaboration.

Physical warm-up In pairs, hold hands and try to pull your partner across the room. With your hands on their shoulders, try to push your partner across room.

Activities Ensure everyone has coloured pens or crayons and Worksheet 15, 'Sports & Games: Tug of Rope':

- ✪ Colour the worksheet with the two teams pulling the rope.
- ✪ This game is often called 'Tug of War' – invent a new name and write it on the sheet.
- ✪ Make two teams and imagine everyone is holding the rope.
- ✪ Work together to make it seem as if the two teams are pulling in opposite directions on the rope.

Sharing Discuss in the whole group how something can be made to look 'real' (for instance, some dances use mime techniques).

Closure Draw a knot in a rope as a promise to yourself in the workbooks; relax with fleeces.

75 Activities I Enjoy: Sports & Games 3

✓ Children ◯ Teenagers

> **Aims** To encourage children to be motivated to participate in physical games and to improve self-confidence.

> **Materials** Large whiteboard & coloured markers, drums, blank paper & folders, workbooks, crayons & coloured pens, mats, fleeces; Worksheet 16 'Sports & Games: Swinging & Running'.

Warm-Up Invite everyone into the circle and allow time for feedback and questions. Explain the aims of the session, which are to choose physical activities and participate in group activity.

Physical warm-up Run around the room and stop, making a shape with the body: it could be a tree, elephant, Ninja, camel, alien, and so on.

Activities Ensure everyone has coloured pens or crayons and Worksheet 16, 'Sports & Games: Swinging & Running':

- ✕ Act out the two activities on the worksheet: run around the room and then pretend to swing on a bar.
- ✕ Move rapidly from one activity to the other.
- ✕ Encourage everyone to choose which of the activities they enjoy more, swinging or running.
- ✕ Colour the preferred activity on the worksheet.

> **Sharing** Talk in the whole group how it felt to do the activity and to draw the activity.

> **Closure** Draw a swing in the workbooks; relax with fleeces.

76 An Activity I Would Like to Do: Games 1

 Children ✓ Teenagers

Aims To encourage group members to explore activities that they may be prevented from doing and to support their choices.

Materials Large whiteboard & coloured markers, drums, blank paper & folders, workbooks, crayons & coloured pens, mats, fleeces.

Warm-Up Invite everyone into the circle and allow time for feedback and questions. Explain the aim of the session, which is to encourage people to make choices regarding physical activities.

Physical warm-up Group members choose a favourite warm-up.

Activities Everyone has paper, crayons and coloured pens. Start a discussion about the Olympic Games and the wide variety of sports involved:

- ☻ In pairs, write or draw as many games as you can think of that are played with a ball.
- ☻ Write or draw as many sports as you can think of that need a hand 'prop', for example: tennis (racquet), throwing sports (javelin, discus), and so on.
- ☻ Write or draw as many sports as you can think of that are played in teams.
- ☻ Write or draw as many sports as you can think of that involve single athletes competing against others.

Sharing Discuss the lists and any sports you had forgotten about; comment on your favourites.

Closure Draw a medal for winning in any sport in your workbooks; relax with fleeces.

 ℗ This page may be photocopied for instructional use only. *101 Activities for Increasing Focus & Motivation* © Sue Jennings 2015

77 An Activity I Would Like to Do: Games 2

○ Children ☑ Teenagers

Aims To encourage opinions about sports and their gender bias.

Materials Large whiteboard & coloured markers, drums, blank paper & folders, workbooks, crayons & coloured pens, mats, fleeces; Worksheet 17 'Sports & Games: Football & Rugby'.

Warm-Up Invite everyone into the circle and allow time for feedback and questions. Explain the aim of the session, which is to consider our choices in games and sport, depending on whether we are male or female.

Physical warm-up Group members choose a warm-up from Resources, Warm-Up Games.

Activities Everyone has coloured pens and Worksheet 17, 'Sports & Games: Football & Rugby':

- ✪ Encourage discussion of boys and girls in sport.
- ✪ Are there sports that girls or boys should not do?
- ✪ Encourage comment on whether individuals admire, for example, girls or women who play football? Are there sports considered too 'female' that a boy would not do?
- ✪ Colour the worksheet and think about the participants who are playing.

Sharing In pairs, discuss sports and games people would like to play, but may feel shy of playing, or during which they fear they might be stopped or ridiculed.

Closure Draw a favourite sport in the workbooks; relax with fleeces.

Activities I Enjoy: Sports & Games

78 An Activity I Would Like to Do: Games 3

 ✓ Children ✓ Teenagers

Aims To encourage imagination and creativity in order to increase motivation.

Materials Large whiteboard & coloured markers, drums, blank paper & folders, workbooks, crayons & coloured pens, mats, fleeces; large pieces of colourful fabric, selection of hats and caps.

Warm-Up Invite everyone into the circle and allow time for feedback and questions. Explain the aim of the session, which is to encourage everyone to develop their own ideas and choices.

Physical warm-up Group members choose a warm-up from Resources, Warm-Up Games.

Activities The pieces of cloth and a selection of hats and caps are made available to the group:

- ✪ Encourage discussion of the 'dramas' that happen in sport: crashes or accidents, unexpected winners, and so on.
- ✪ In small groups, choose a dramatic 'incident' from sport.
- ✪ Decide how to make it into a short play, with or without words.
- ✪ Use the hats and cloth to help create the characters.

Sharing Present the plays to whole group; give and receive feedback.

Closure Draw and colour a star in the workbooks; relax with fleeces.

79 An Activity I Would Like to Do: Games 4

 ✓ Children ✓ Teenagers

Aims To encourage imagination and creativity in order to increase motivation.

Materials Large whiteboard & coloured markers, drums, blank paper & folders, workbooks, crayons & coloured pens, mats, fleeces; colourful cloths, hats and caps, winners' shields, trophies or medals.

Warm-Up Invite everyone into the circle and allow time for feedback and questions. Explain the aim of the session, which is to create fantasy situations based on activities that people would like to do.

Physical warm-up Everyone walks around the room as if they are in a dream or a nightmare; interact with others in their dreams.

Activities Have the cloths, caps, winners' shields, trophies or medals available to help the group dramatise a sporting event that is unlikely to happen:

- ✪ In small groups, think of a 'dream' sport that the group would be unlikely to win.
- ✪ Create a fantasy scene in which someone wins the competition (or the match) and is presented with a medal or shield by a famous person.
- ✪ Practise it several times, changing over roles so that everyone has the experience of winning.
- ✪ Share the scenes with the whole group.

Sharing Discuss in whole group how it felt to play the winner.

Closure Draw a 'dream' sport in the workbooks; relax with fleeces.

80 An Activity I Would Like to Do: Board Game

 Children  Teenagers

> **Aims** To give everyone the opportunity to win a board-game championship in order to encourage self-confidence and motivation.

> **Materials** Large whiteboard & coloured markers, drums, blank paper & folders, workbooks, crayons & coloured pens, mats, fleeces; medals.

Warm-Up Invite everyone into the circle and allow time for feedback and questions. Explain the aims of the session, which are to create a board-game activity and role play being a champion in order to build up confidence.

Physical warm-up Choose a warm-up from Resources, Warm-Up Games.

Activities Discuss in the group any favourite board game, for example 'Operation', 'Monopoly', 'Cluedo', scrabble and chess:

- ⊗ Discuss how most board games are played quietly, and compare this with the noise of team games.
- ⊗ In small groups, choose a game and create a scene about a championship, with everyone swapping roles.
- ⊗ Decide on an incident that happens during the game and modify the scene.
- ⊗ Play the scenes for the rest of the group, both the championship and the incident.

> **Sharing** Give feedback to each other about the scenes and discuss everyone's favourite roles.

> **Closure** Draw an object from a board game in the workbooks; relax with fleeces.

Part Nine
Activities I Enjoy: Hobbies & Interests

The aim of this section is to stimulate interests in activities apart from sport. Not all young people are interested in sporting activities, even if they have the physical confidence to become involved, and another type of hobby or interest may suit them better. Collecting objects of various sorts encourages patience and the capacity to wait, rather than expecting instant results. Collecting can also give young people a sense of their own history if they are collecting old objects.

Collectors need to acquire information about their collections and to find ways of organising and storing the things they collect. This can also be a social activity, as individuals can meet to exchange objects and information. Car-boot sales, house clearances and eBay are all sources for acquiring new objects. However, an initial passion can flag and become lost very quickly; the challenge may be to encourage and support young people in sustained, long-term interests, pursued at a gentler pace.

Activities

81 I am Interested in … 1

82 I am Interested in … 2

83 I am Interested in … 3

84 I am Interested in … 4

85 I am Interested in … 5

86 I am Interested in …6

87 Change in Direction 1

88 Change in Direction 2

89 Change in Direction 3

90 Change in Direction 4

Worksheets

18 Activities I Enjoy: Collections

81 I am Interested in ... 1

☑ Children ☑ Teenagers

Aims To encourage interest in new ideas and subjects.

Materials Large whiteboard & coloured markers, drums, blank paper & folders, workbooks, crayons & coloured pens, mats, fleeces.

Warm-Up Invite everyone into the circle and allow time for feedback and questions. Explain the aims of the session, which are to discover new ideas and subjects and to encourage fresh interests.

Physical warm-up Take it in turns to mime a hobby without using words: group members guess what it is.

Activities Use the whiteboard to facilitate discussion and supply each person with blank paper and coloured pens or crayons:

⊗ Start a discussion regarding hobbies and interests; encourage group members to call out ideas and write them on the whiteboard.

⊗ Start to group the ideas under different headings: games, collections, art and craft, and so on.

⊗ Point out how many traditional hobbies are more difficult these days, for instance stamp collecting because of franking machines.

⊗ Everyone draws a picture of a hobby or interest that they had not thought of before this session.

Sharing In small groups, look at the pictures and discuss the reality of starting a new interest.

Closure Draw a picture that describes a hobby in the workbooks; relax with fleeces.

82 I am Interested in ... 2

☑ Children   ☑ Teenagers

Aims To stimulate interest in new ideas and activities from the past.

Materials Large whiteboard & coloured markers, drums, blank paper & folders, workbooks, crayons & coloured pens, mats, fleeces; pictures of old-fashioned (even medieval!) games and activities.

Warm-Up Invite everyone into the circle and allow time for feedback and questions. Explain the aim of the session, which is to explore how children and teenagers in the past spent their time.

Physical warm-up Group members choose a warm-up from Resources, Warm-Up Games.

Activities Use the whiteboard to facilitate discussion and supply each person with blank paper and coloured pens or crayons:

- Use pictures to give a short talk about games and activities from the past: hobby horses, shuttlecock, 'Nine Men's Morris', and so on. List them on the whiteboard.
- Discuss whether these are still played or if there are modern equivalents; what are the modern versions like?
- Encourage the idea that there have always been games and playing.
- Everyone draws and colours an old-fashioned game.

Sharing In pairs, compare pictures and discuss the possibilities of playing the games.

Closure Draw an old-fashioned hobby horse in the workbooks; relax with fleeces.

83 I am Interested in... 3

☑ Children ☑ Teenagers

Aims To encourage interest in new activities and to explore these dramatically.

Materials Large whiteboard & coloured markers, drums, blank paper & folders, workbooks, crayons & coloured pens, mats, fleeces; pictures of traditional games.

Warm-Up Invite everyone into the circle and allow time for feedback and questions. Explain the aim of the session, which is to explore traditional games and sports

Physical warm-up Play imaginary games of hopscotch in small groups.

Activities Remind the group that traditional communities did not have technology, Wi-Fi, TV and so on. How did young people pass the time? (When they were not needed to work in the fields, farms and factories!):

- ✪ In small groups, recreate an old-fashioned game.
- ✪ Decide on where this is being played: in a village, in a town?
- ✪ Put all the games together as a 'day in the life' of this community.
- ✪ Use them as the basis for a documentary drama about this community.

Sharing Discuss your ideas in the whole group, and compare life in the older community with that in a modern community.

Closure Write or draw special words from the drama in the workbooks; relax with fleeces.

84 I am Interested in ... 4

☑ Children ☑ Teenagers

> **Aims** To stimulate interest in new sorts of hobbies and activities.

> **Materials** Large whiteboard & coloured markers, drums, blank paper & folders, workbooks, crayons & coloured pens, mats, fleeces; visual aids to represent different kinds of collections, if available, Worksheet 18 'Activities I Enjoy: Collections'.

Warm-Up Invite everyone into the circle and allow time for feedback and questions. Explain the aims of the session, which are to think about hobbies and interests and perhaps choose a new activity to develop.

Physical warm-up Group members choose a warm-up from Resources, Warm-Up Games.

Activities Use the whiteboard and markers to facilitate discussion; everyone has coloured pens or crayons and a copy of Worksheet 18, 'Activities I Enjoy: Collections':

- ✪ Open up a discussion about the things people collect (with visual aids if available).
- ✪ Invite suggestions from everyone and write them on the board.
- ✪ Acknowledge that some collecting hobbies can be expensive!
- ✪ Fill the circle on the worksheet with interesting objects that could be collected, then write three words about your collection in the spaces.

> **Sharing** Compare collections in pairs and talk about your real interests.

> **Closure** Draw or write something about an object from your collection in the workbooks; relax with fleeces.

85 I am Interested in ... 5

☑ Children ◯ Teenagers

Aims To stimulate greater awareness of choices and interests.

Materials Large whiteboard & coloured markers, drums, blank paper & folders, workbooks, crayons & coloured pens, mats, fleeces; selections of objects that could form collections (miniature toys, stamps, shells, small gemstones, foreign coins).

Warm-Up Invite everyone into the circle and allow time for feedback and questions. Explain the aim of the session, which is to stimulate and rekindle interest in potential activities.

Physical warm-up Group members choose a singing game or activity to play in the circle.

Activities Provide blank paper for each person and a selection of small objects that might be collected:

- ✪ Everyone chooses one set of small objects and places them on the paper.
- ✪ Explore objects and arrange them patterns or shapes.
- ✪ Change seats and explore another person's set of objects.
- ✪ Change and explore three or four times.

Sharing Talk with a partner and compare the objects you liked and disliked.

Closure Draw and colour your favourite objects in the workbooks; relax with fleeces.

86 I am Interested in ... 6

⬭ Children ☑ Teenagers

Aims To encourage and stimulate the consideration and choice of new interests.

Materials Large whiteboard & coloured markers, drums, blank paper & folders, workbooks, crayons & coloured pens, mats, fleeces; collections of small gems and stones (available cheaply online or in 'New Age' shops).

Warm-Up Invite everyone into the circle and allow time for feedback and questions. Explain the aims of the session, which are to explore new ideas for interests and to encourage everyone to consider new possibilities.

Physical warm-up Group members choose a warm-up from Resources, Warm-Up Games.

Activities Each person has blank paper and coloured pens or crayons. Lay out collections of gems and stones for everyone to explore:

- ✪ Encourage discussion of different gems and stones, their names and origins.
- ✪ Allow exploration of different groups of stones, their textures and colours.
- ✪ Identify stones that are called birthstones, and encourage group members to find out the attributes of their own birthstones.
- ✪ Share stories about stones and those considered to bring good luck and ill luck.

Sharing Allow everyone to choose one gemstone for themselves and discuss their preferences in the group.

Closure Draw a container or a bag for a gemstone in the workbooks; relax with fleeces.

87 Change in Direction 1

☑ Children ☑ Teenagers

Aims To encourage a refocus in a new direction and to 'try something out'.

Materials Large whiteboard & coloured markers, drums, blank paper & folders, workbooks, crayons & coloured pens, mats, fleeces; wooden or plastic boards for modelling, 'Modroc' for modelling (plaster of Paris bandage), pots of water or spray water bottles; acrylic paints and white glue (if wished).

Warm-Up Invite everyone into the circle and allow time for feedback and questions. Explain the aims of the session, which are to try something different and to create a model of any object.

Physical warm-up A focussed stretch, up and out, breathing deeply; then shake out all the limbs and stretch again.

Activities Give each person a modelling board, several pieces of Modroc and a water bottle or spray (the water can also be shared):

- ✪ Explain that after the Modroc has been damped with water it will dry out again quickly, so it needs to be regularly redamped.
- ✪ Encourage everyone to make whatever they wish with the Modroc; a free-form shape, or a sculpture, or a copy of an object.
- ✪ Smooth the finished object so that there is a thin film of plaster covering the surface.
- ✪ Squeeze away any surplus water and leave to dry.

Note that once the Modroc is thoroughly dry (you can speed this up with a hairdryer if necessary), it can be painted with acrylic paint. When the paint has dried, seal the surface with a thin coating of white glue.

Sharing Discuss the art-making in the whole group and explain that another session can be used for painting the models.

Closure Draw the models in the workbooks; relax with fleeces.

88 Change in Direction 2

☑ Children ☑ Teenagers

> **Aims** To continue to refocus on new directions and trying things out.

> **Materials** Large whiteboard & coloured markers, drums, blank paper & folders, workbooks, crayons & coloured pens, mats, fleeces; boards for modelling, blank plastic masks, pots or tubes of Vaseline, 'Modroc' (plaster of Paris bandage) for modelling, water pots or spray bottles, scissors; acrylic paints and white glue (if wished).

Warm-Up Invite everyone into the circle and allow time for feedback and questions. Explain the aim of the session, which is to continue to refocus on new activities.

Physical warm-up A focussed stretch, up and out, breathing deeply; shake out all the limbs and stretch again.

Activities Give each person a modelling board, a blank mask and Vaseline, several pieces of Modroc, scissors and a water bottle or spray (the water can also be shared):

- ✪ Thinly coat the mask with Vaseline; cut the Modroc into matchbox-sized squares.
- ✪ Damp the Modroc and build up three layers on the mask, damping again if necessary; allow the mask to dry.
- ✪ Gently peel the Modroc away from the masks and wipe off any Vaseline remaining on the back.
- ✪ Trim any rough edges away from the Modroc mask, including around the eyes; decide whether to cut out a mouth.
- ✪ Use a thick needle to make holes either side, and then thread elastic through the holes so that the mask may be worn on the face. Alternatively make a hole at the base to take a stick for holding the mask against the face.

Note that the masks can be painted in a subsequent session (use acrylic paints sealed with white glue, as suggested in Activity 87), and wool or string can be stuck or threaded for hair.

> **Sharing** Discuss the masks in the whole group, and ask if group members wish to paint or otherwise add to their masks in a second session.

> **Closure** Colour a design for your mask in the workbooks; relax with fleeces.

89 Change in Direction 3

☑ Children ☑ Teenagers

Aims To build on the mask experience of previous sessions and to encourage the acquisition of new skills.

Materials Large whiteboard & coloured markers, drums, blank paper & folders, workbooks, crayons & coloured pens, mats, fleeces; masks made in previous sessions, large pieces of cloth.

Warm-Up Invite everyone into the circle and allow time for feedback and questions. Explain the aims of the session, which are to actually use the masks and to develop drama ideas.

Physical warm-up Running, walking, jumping, waving, to focus energy.

Activities Each person has their own mask (either mounted on a stick or secured with elastic). Supply plenty of cloth for clothing props and use drums to dramatise the activity:

- ✪ Practice walking and moving wearing the mask; create bigger eye holes or a breathing hole if this is awkward.
- ✪ Think about the character of the mask and the story they have to tell.
- ✪ In groups of three, create a drama with the masks, cloths and drums.
- ✪ Show the drama to the whole group.

Sharing Discuss how wearing masks can encourage confidence and the ability to take on new roles.

Closure Draw a mask in the workbooks; relax with fleeces.

Activities I Enjoy: Hobbies & Interests

90 Change in Direction 4

☑ Children   ☑ Teenagers

Aims To develop the creative ideas of the whole group in order to build cooperation and artistic skills.

Materials Large whiteboard & coloured markers, drums, blank paper & folders, workbooks, crayons & coloured pens, mats, fleeces; masks and cloths.

Warm-Up Invite everyone into the circle and allow time for feedback and questions. Explain the aims of the session, which are to encourage group ideas and creative skills.

Physical warm-up Group members decide on warm-ups.

Activities Everyone has their mask; make cloth props and drums available to help with dramatisation:

- ✷ Encourage whole group discussion of potential themes for a masked drama.
- ✷ Improvisation without masks can stimulate new ideas that may then be worked on in smaller groups.
- ✷ Experiment without words, using only movement and drumming.
- ✷ Put all the threads together and perform a drama, wearing masks, cloths and using drums.

Sharing Discuss the performance with the whole group and how it felt.

Closure Write several words to express the experience in the workbooks; relax with fleeces.

Part Ten
Using Stories

Stories in all their forms contribute a very important dimension to people's lives. Almost everyone enjoys a 'good yarn', and there are many opportunities to tell or listen to stories. It is simple, available and sociable. Storytelling brings people together in formal and informal settings, from the spontaneous to the planned, from the intimately social to the public. We construct our conversations in narrative form – 'one thing leads to another' – and people who participate get a sense of well-being from sharing a story.

Storytelling is very ancient: many cultures tell their origins through stories and may have especially designated storytellers. History is passed from generation to generation through oral culture, and people gain security from a sense of belonging.

People who have difficulty in concentrating will often find security in the world of stories. A story provides a structure that usually has a beginning, middle and end. Most people learn stories even before they are born; a sense of narrative is experienced as mothers spontaneously tell tales both during pregnancy and in the early weeks and months of the baby's life. If this has not taken place, some people will have difficulties with structure and sequence. Rhythm and story are probably the two most important resources for children and teenagers who have come adrift.

Cartoon stories are a first step to creating a story without words and are invaluable as starters for those struggling with creating narratives. A simple sequence involves filling in four squares with the following pictures:

1 Think of a character; draw it in square 1.
2 The character does something; draw it in square 2.
3 Something happens; draw it in square 3.
4 How does it end? Draw it in square 4.

This basic structure encourages sequencing ('one thing leading to another') and creates the framework of beginning, middle and end. The activity can act as a warm-up, to which words are added when the picture is told as a story. Then it might be possible to write down key words on the whiteboard, giving verbal life to each person's cartoon.

Although the four squares and what to draw inside them can be illustrated on the board, refrain from showing an actual cartoon. Most group members will then just copy it, in an attempt to appear 'right'!

Activities

91 Cartoon Tales 1

92 Cartoon Tales 2

93 Myths & Stories 1

94 Myths & Stories 2

95 Myths & Stories 3

96 Myths & Stories 4

97 Myths & Stories 5

98 Myths & Stories 6

99 Journey through the Course 1

100 Journey through the Course 2

101 Certificate & Celebration

Worksheets

20 Group Contract

21 Certificate of Achievement

Story Sheets

2 The Shepherd Boy and Weaving Maiden

3 The Broken Promise: The Mulberry Tree

91 Cartoon Tales 1

☑ Children ☑ Teenagers

> **Aims** To encourage narratives in words or pictures in order to promote 'movement' in thinking and creating and to develop sequencing.

> **Materials** Large whiteboard & coloured markers, drums, blank paper & folders, workbooks, crayons & coloured pens, mats, fleeces.

Warm-Up Invite everyone into the circle and allow time for feedback and questions. Explain the aim of the session, which is to create basic stories through cartoon pictures in order to develop confidence in storytelling.

Physical warm-up Members of the group decide on their own warm-up.

Activities Everyone has blank paper and coloured pens or crayons. Invite group members to divide their paper in four by folding or drawing lines; explain that cartoons can follow the four steps as described in the Introduction to Part Ten:

- ✪ Think of a cartoon character – one that exists or invent a new one.
- ✪ In the first square draw the character and where they live.
- ✪ In the second square draw something the character does.
- ✪ In the third square draw something that happens.
- ✪ In the fourth square draw how it ends.

> **Sharing** Tell the story of your cartoon to a partner.

> **Closure** Draw a cartoon character in the workbooks; relax with fleeces.

Using Stories

92 Cartoon Tales 2

☑ Children ☑ Teenagers

Aims To develop sequencing in simple narratives and to add single words.

Materials Large whiteboard & coloured markers, drums, blank paper & folders, workbooks, crayons & coloured pens, mats, fleeces.

Warm-Up Invite everyone into the circle and allow time for feedback and questions. Explain the aim of the session, which is to practise storytelling through using cartoons.

Physical warm-up Group members choose a physical warm-up. Go on to practise typical cartoon words: 'splat', 'ker-boom', 'eek', and so on. Encourage group members to contribute their own ideas.

Activities Everyone has blank paper and coloured pens or crayons. Ask group members to divide their paper in four by folding or drawing lines; explain that cartoons can follow the four steps (see the Introduction to Part Ten). Invite everyone to think of a cartoon character, either one that already exists or one of their own invention, and to repeat all the cartoon words from the warm-up (write the words on the board):

✪ Draw the character in square 1, and what they are doing in square 2.

✪ Something happens in square 3, and the ending goes in square 4.

✪ Look at the story and think of one word the character(s) are saying.

✪ Write one word for each character in a balloon coming out of their mouth; this can be one from the board or another of your choice.

Sharing Share cartoon with a partner and see how many words from the board have been used.

Closure Write two cartoon words in the workbooks; relax with fleeces.

Using Stories

93 Myths & Stories 1

✓ Children ✓ Teenagers

> **Aims** To explore stories and their outcomes through imaginative and unusual tales from other cultures.

> **Materials** Large whiteboard & coloured markers, drums, blank paper & folders, workbooks, crayons & coloured pens, mats, fleeces; Story Sheet 2 'The Shepherd Boy & the Weaving Maiden'.

Warm-Up Invite everyone into the circle and allow time for feedback and questions. Explain the aim of the session, which is to explore stories that are unusual and can help us with creativity and concentration.

Physical warm-up Imagine you are a farmer's boy or girl on any sort of farm. Improvise any activities on the farm, and then develop these with a partner. Imagine you are someone who weaves beautiful material; improvise any weaving actions on your own and then with a partner.

Activities Everyone has paper, coloured pens or crayons and Story Sheet 2, 'The Shepherd Boy & the Weaving Maiden':

- ⊗ Read the story aloud to the group and invite comments.
- ⊗ Invite everyone to colour the stars and flowers.
- ⊗ Draw a shepherd boy or a girl who is weaving.
- ⊗ Draw the landscape where they are working.

> **Sharing** Show the pictures in the whole group and encourage thoughts about the story.

> **Closure** Draw a black crow in the workbooks; relax with fleeces.

Using Stories

94 Myths & Stories 2

 Children ☑ Teenagers

> **Aims** To explore the feelings behind stories through drawing and dancing in order to better understand our own feelings.

> **Materials** Large whiteboard & coloured markers, drums, blank paper & folders, workbooks, crayons & coloured pens, mats, fleeces; Story Sheet 2 'The Shepherd Boy & the Weaving Maiden', stiff card and scissors, sticks (for the masks).

Warm-Up Invite everyone into the circle and allow time for feedback and questions. Explain the aim of the session, which is to explore a story from another culture to see what it can help us to understand about our own.

Physical warm-up Invite everyone to move as a shepherd boy chasing his sheep, weave as a maiden weaving silk, fly as the crows, walk as the angry father, brandishing his stick. Allow all the movements to become exaggerated, then let them lead into dancing the characters.

Activities Everyone has stiff card, scissors, coloured pens or crayons, a stick (plastic rod or dowel) and Story Sheet 2, 'The Shepherd Boy & the Weaving Maiden':

- ✪ Read the story through and everyone chooses a character.
- ✪ Draw a mask of the character on the card.
- ✪ Colour it, cut it out, and attach the stick in order to hold it.
- ✪ Walk as the character around the room holding the mask.

> **Sharing** Show the mask to the whole group and talk about the character.

> **Closure** Draw the golden cow in the workbooks; relax with fleeces.

Using Stories

Myths & Stories 3

☑ Children   ☑ Teenagers

Aims To explore the concept of patience.

Materials Large whiteboard & coloured markers, drums, blank paper & folders, workbooks, crayons & coloured pens, mats, fleeces; Story Sheet 2 'The Shepherd Boy & the Weaving Maiden'.

Warm-Up Invite everyone into the circle and allow time for feedback and questions. Explain the aim of the session, which is to explore the theme of having to wait and how that might feel.

Physical warm-up Walk very calmly around room; then walk very impatiently around the room. In pairs, one person says, 'You must!', and the other says, 'I can't!' Allow the dialogue to build into an impatient scene, then change roles.

Activities Everyone has Story Sheet 2, 'The Shepherd Boy & the Weaving Maiden', and follows it while the story is read out loud (by a participant or the facilitator):

- ✪ Encourage discussion on the theme of waiting and frustration.
- ✪ In pairs or small groups, think of a modern scene based on the 'waiting' theme.
- ✪ Create a drama without using words, or by using body sculpts (see Introduction, How to Structure a Session: Explanation of core techniques).
- ✪ Share the dramas in the whole group.

This exercise can be repeated using words if the group feel confident to do so.

Sharing In whole group discuss the theme of waiting, throughout history and in our own day.

Closure Draw a star in the workbooks; relax with fleeces.

Using Stories

96 Myths & Stories 4

 Children ✓ Teenagers

Aims To encourage understanding of the emotions we feel when we are 'let down' or someone breaks a promise.

Materials Large whiteboard & coloured markers, drums, blank paper & folders, workbooks, crayons & coloured pens, mats, fleeces; Story Sheet 3 'The Broken Promise: The Mulberry Tree'.

Warm-Up Invite everyone into the circle and allow time for feedback and questions. Explain the aim of the session, which is to think about how we feel when someone lets us down or breaks a promise they have made – or how we feel when we break a promise ourselves.

Physical warm-up In threes, two people are bandits and the third is being chased: chase and capture without actual touching. Everyone tries out different roles.

Activities Each person has coloured pens or crayons and Story Sheet 3, 'The Broken Promise: The Mulberry Tree':

- ✪ Read the story aloud and invite discussion.
- ✪ Remind people that this is a mythical story, something other-worldly and not about our everyday lives.
- ✪ Colour the worksheet.
- ✪ Answer the questions through words or drawings.

Sharing Working in pairs, discuss the story and your answers.

Closure Draw a horse in the workbooks; relax with fleeces.

97 Myths & Stories 5

☑ Children ☑ Teenagers

> **Aims** To encourage reflection on the consequences of our actions and the fact that everything we do has a consequence.

> **Materials** Large whiteboard & coloured markers, drums, blank paper & folders, workbooks, crayons & coloured pens, mats, fleeces; Story Sheet 3 'The Broken Promise: The Mulberry Tree'.

Warm-Up   Invite everyone into the circle and allow time for feedback and questions. Explain the aims of the session, which are to consider what happens when promises are broken and to understand that everything we do in life has consequences.

Physical warm-up   In pairs, lead your partner around the room on an imaginary thread at least two arms' lengths away. (This requires lot of concentration in order to maintain the same distance between the two people!) Change roles.

Activities   Give everyone a copy of Story Sheet 3, 'The Broken Promise: The Mulberry Tree'. Someone reads the story aloud (this could be either a group member or the facilitator):

- ✪ Share how it feels to be let down or to have promises broken.
- ✪ In small groups, choose someone's personal experience and turn it into a scene.
- ✪ Create three or four body sculpts (see Introduction, How to Structure a Session: Explanation of core techniques).
- ✪ Show the scene to the whole group.

The scenes may be enacted with or without words, depending on the group's level of confidence.

> **Sharing** Discuss the scenes in the whole group, supporting group members who shared their personal stories.

> **Closure** Draw a friendship knot in the workbooks; relax with fleeces.

Using Stories

98 Myths & Stories 6

 Children ✓ Teenagers

Aims To encourage participants to take creative steps in their narratives and to develop their own ideas.

Materials Large whiteboard & coloured markers, drums, blank paper & folders, workbooks, crayons & coloured pens, mats, fleeces.

Warm-Up Invite everyone into the circle and allow time for feedback and questions. Explain the aim of the session, which is to encourage participants to develop their own ideas about stories.

Physical warm-up Group members decide on warm-ups that have some connection with stories they know.

Activities Everyone has blank paper and coloured pens or crayons. Encourage group members to call out the titles of stories that they know, perhaps from the TV or that they have been told in this project or in other classes:

- ✪ Write the main events in the stories on the board, using the four-step sequence described in the Introduction to this section.
- ✪ Encourage participants to work in pairs and create their own story, using some of the elements from the stories on the board.
- ✪ Draw the sequence of the story or create it in cartoon form.
- ✪ Tell the story to another pair.

Sharing Share your stories with whole group and compare similarities and differences. What constitutes a good story?

Closure Draw a book in the workbooks; relax with fleeces.

Using Stories

99 Journey through the Course 1

☑ Children ☑ Teenagers

Aims To process everyone's journey through the course and encourage them to understand sequences in their own activities.

Materials Large whiteboard & coloured markers, drums, blank paper & folders, workbooks, crayons & coloured pens, mats, fleeces.

Warm-Up Invite everyone into the circle and allow time for feedback and questions. Explain the aims of the session, which are to think about the group experience of this project and to consider how different themes have developed.

Physical warm-up Encourage members to create an improvised obstacle race across different landscapes.

Activities Everyone has folder containing their course work, blank paper and coloured pens or crayons:

- ✪ Allow time for discussion and write the key stages of the project on the board.
- ✪ Give people time to look at the contents of their folders in sequence.
- ✪ Create a closing sheet with pictures that show things learned in the course of the project.
- ✪ Decorate the page with favourite colours and patterns.

Sharing Show the sheets to the group and compare similarities.

Closure Draw a decorated medal in the workbooks; relax with fleeces.

Using Stories

100 Journey through the Course 2

☑ Children ☑ Teenagers

> **Aims** To bring the programme or project to a close and acknowledge important changes in feelings and learning.

> **Materials** Large whiteboard & coloured markers, drums, blank paper & folders, workbooks, crayons & coloured pens, mats, fleeces.

Warm-Up Invite everyone into the circle and allow time for feedback and questions. Explain the aims of the session, which are to acknowledge the closing of the group and to share important learning on the way.

Physical warm-up Group members lead favourite warm-ups that have been learnt on the project.

Activities Everyone has their workbooks, coloured pens or crayons and blank paper. Write the main stages of the programme or project on the board:

- ✪ Invite everyone to read through their workbooks and consider personal changes.
- ✪ Think about things that have not changed and might be disappointments.
- ✪ Think about the best thing that happened on the project.
- ✪ Write or draw all of these words in the workbooks: 'personal changes', 'disappointments', 'best thing of all'.

> **Sharing** Discuss any disappointments in the whole group, and make suggestions for ways in which the course could be improved another time.

> **Closure** Choose a final picture to draw in the workbooks; relax with fleeces.

101 Certificate & Celebration

✓ Children   ✓ Teenagers

Aims To acknowledge and celebrate the achievements of all group members and to affirm their success.

Materials Large whiteboard & coloured markers, drums, blank paper & folders, workbooks, crayons & coloured pens, mats, fleeces; Worksheet 21 'Certificate of Achievement', completed for each person.

Warm-Up Invite everyone into the circle and allow time for feedback and questions. Explain the aims of the session, which are to celebrate everyone's success in the group project and to have a final session to acknowledge every individual and their progress.

Physical warm-up Group members choose warm-up games that are suitable for a party atmosphere.

Activities Create an atmosphere of celebration and hand out Worksheet 21, 'Certificate of Achievement', to each person:

- ☣ Encourage group members to choose creative activities they enjoy.
- ☣ Use any of the resources such as the drums.
- ☣ If possible take photographs of everyone being presented with their certificate.
- ☣ Make sure that everyone has been acknowledged individually before they leave.

Sharing Everything in this session is sharing!

Closure Make sure that everyone takes their workbook home with them.

Using Stories

Resources

Warm-Up Games

Worksheets

1   Feelings to Express & Change

2   Actions that Show Feelings & Change

3   Decisions I Want to Make

4a & 4b   Distracting Sounds

5a & 5b   Distracting Smells

6a & 6b   Distracting Sights

7a & 7b   Distracting Memories

8a & 8b   Distracting Fears

9a & 9b   Distracting Worries

10a & 10b   Distracting Feelings

11a & 11b   Distracting Disappointments

12a & 12b   Distracting Excitements

13   The Heart Tree

14   Activities I Enjoy: Sport

15   Sports & Games: Tug of Rope

16   Sports & Games: Swinging & Running

17   Sports & Games: Football & Rugby

18 Activities I Enjoy: Collections

19 Template for Dice

20 Group Agreement

21 Certificate of Achievement

Story Sheets

1 A Midsummer Night's Dream

2 The Shepherd Boy & the Weaving Maiden

3 The Broken Promise: The Mulberry Tree

References & Further Reading

Resources

Warm-Up Games

These exercises vary from very simple to more complex games. They are ideal as an introduction to 'action learning', and provide a basis for confidence building. A warm-up is just that, it warms up the body and the brain, ready for creative activity. Perhaps their most important function is simply to focus energy. It is important, when choosing warm-ups, that they are linked to the activities in the group and not chosen at random.

I usually start with physical warm-ups, because often there is surplus energy that needs to be focussed and then transformed. My approach does not work with, for example, angry expression for its own sake, in the sense of smashing old china or breaking bricks; I use physical energy that expresses angry energy, and then turns it into something more positive.

For example, a physical game of throwing and catching the soft ball focuses scattered energy and allows it to become collaborative energy. A jog around the park enhances the 'feel-good' factor, and prepares group members for focussed group work. In all warm-ups it is important to remember awareness of breathing, whether to create energy or to bring about relaxation.

1 Breathing and voice
(Exercises to be repeated 3 or 4 times.)

1 Breathe in through the nose to a count of 4, and then out through the mouth to a count of 4; keep the shoulders relaxed and the tummy tucked in. Repeat, with a pause for 4 counts between breathing in and out.
2 Take a deep breath in through the nose, and breathe out on the word 'home'.
3 Say 'ho, ho, ho', as loudly as possible. Repeat, increasing volume; and then repeat, becoming quieter.
4 Repeat quickly, 'red leather, yellow leather', 5 times, then 10 times.
5 Repeat quickly, 'a clown with a crown', 5 times, then 10 times.
6 Talk a nonsense language with a partner as fast as possible, and then very slowly as if feeling sleepy.

2 Strong movement

1 Invite the group to scatter around the room and call out 'freeze!'; everyone stands absolutely still. Then call out, 'go!'; everyone moves again. Repeat several times until unison is achieved.

2 Suggest contrasting movements, such as running around in a circle and scattering all over the place.

3 Move around the room as if being blown.

4 Run around and jump very high.

5 Stand absolutely still and create a silence.

3 Rhythm and drum work

1 Invite the group to sit in a circle and clap a simple rhythm until they are clapping in unison.

2 Divide the group in half: one half clapping at the original speed, the other twice as fast.

3 Play with the idea of different rhythms; invite the group to make suggestions.

4 Allow group members to use a drum and lead the rhythm; the person with the drum leads and the group copies.

5 Use a drumming CD, and suggest that everyone copies a rhythm.

4 More rhythm and drum work

1 Using a drumbeat, suggest everyone walks to the beat.

2 Try marching to the drumbeat, first on the spot, and then around the room

3 March with a partner and synchronise the movements.

4 March with three people and create the marching 'wheel', in which the person at the centre of the wheel marches on the spot, while the others move around in a circle. (Quite a challenge!)

5 Attempt to march backwards, staying in the wheel. (A big challenge!)

5 Physical work

1 Throw the soft ball between group members, while running around the room; vary between throwing the ball randomly, and shouting the name of the person who should catch it.

2 Hold hands in a circle and pull one way, then the other, keeping the circle intact.

3 Hold hands in a circle, and then move over and under everyone until a tight knot is formed. Slowly undo the knot without letting go of the hands.

4 Pass a clap or a rhythm around the circle to create a ripple effect, as if the sound is continuous.

5 Stand in a circle; each person sits down one at a time, but if two go down at the same time, everyone has to start from the beginning. Repeat the exercise, this time standing up from sitting.

6 Synchronised games

1 Everyone stands in a large circle; each person takes one step forward, but if two people move at the same time, the game starts again.

2 Repeat the exercise, this time moving out of the circle, one step at a time.

3 Everyone stands in a large circle and counts, 'one, two, three, four'. On 'four' each person looks at someone else; if the same person is also looking at them, they change places. Keep repeating until there has been plenty of movement across the group.

4 Variation: number everyone in the group (just go around the circle and have each person say their number); call out two numbers and those people have to change places.

5 More difficult: call out two sets of numbers, such as '2 and 7' and '4 and 8'. Those four people change places, with everyone taking care not to bump into the others as they cross the circle.

7 Clapping and rhythm

1 Pass a single clap around the circle, one person following the next and keeping up the rhythm.

2 Repeat in the opposite direction, varying the pace if group is ready.

3 Change to a double clap and send it around in one direction.

4 Vary the pace and send in the opposite direction

5 Change to a triple clap and send it in one direction; at the same time send a double clap in the opposite direction.

8 Rhythm in words and music

1 Share the idea that certain jobs have their own rhythmic chant, so that everyone works together, for example: pulling a rope, rowing a boat.

2 Invite everyone to sit in the circle and teach the chant: 'Aayee oh, aayee oh, ay, ay, ay, ay, aayee oh.' Practise until synchronised.

3 Add the movement of rowing a boat to the rhythm; practise until the chant and movement are synchronised.

4 Explain to the group that words used together in a sentence have a rhythm. Invite members to think of famous, rhythmic catchphrases, such as: 'It's goodnight from him – and goodnight from me'; or 'Nice to see you – to see you nice'.

5 Ask the group to think about the rhythms in music and song lyrics. Invite group members to think of music they like with a strong rhythm and words, and practise it together.

9 Rhyming words and rhythmic words

(Use one of the rhyming dictionaries suggested in Resources, 'References & Further Reading'.)

1 Invite the group to sit in the circle and clap, while saying words that rhyme, for example: 'splat, mat, cat, rat'; or 'hi, my, try, cry, fry'.

2 Share words that have a strong rhythm, such as: 'dinner, dinner, dinner'; or 'hokey, cokey, cokey, cokey'.

3 Invite everyone to make up two lines that rhyme, for example: 'I went to school, and broke a rule'; or 'I went to school, and fell in a pool.' Encourage more and more nonsense, such as: 'I went to school, riding a mule.'

4 In pairs, write down (or just say) as many words as possible that rhyme with 'song' (one rhyming dictionary lists 21). Then add slight pronunciation variations, for example, 'tongue'.

5 Give group members working in pairs a first line, such as: 'Today I am going to cook a song.' Each pair adds three more lines.

10 Drama and focus games

1 'Varoom': With everyone standing in a circle, one person calls 'Varoom', and looks at someone else. That person says 'Varoom' to another, and so on. There's no 'varooming' someone next to you, and no repetition back and forth to same person.

2 'Varoom Plus': 'Varoom' someone in the group, who then chooses to call 'Bazooka', and to hold both their arms in front of them, hands clasped, pointing towards someone on the opposite side of group. Or they can call out 'Varoom Plus', at which everyone crosses their arms on their chest. The leader starts 'Varoom Plus' again

3 Variation: As above, but adding a third action and sound: 'Lalala'. If someone shouts 'Lalala', everyone has to put their hands over their ears and shout, 'Lalala' four times!

4 Invite members of the group to add an action with a nonsense word, but ask them to avoid movements that could involve hitting other people; try to keep all extended movement in front, rather than to the side, of the body.

5 Invite members of the group to choose one of the games to practise very quickly.

11 More drama and focus games

1 'Bees Knees': Everyone runs around the room with one hand on one knee, calling out 'Bees Knees'. Each person has to touch four pairs of knees; then retrace steps and find and touch the knees touched the first time.

2 'Aliens': Everyone stands in a circle. The leader is in the middle and turns around slowly, then points with clasped hands towards one person, calling 'Medan'. The person who has been pointed at is an 'alien' and has to duck down on one knee. The two people on either side of the 'alien' face each other and call out 'Nimro'. The 'alien' between them (still ducking) calls back 'Feelib', and can then stand up again. *However*, if anyone says the wrong word, they have to stay on one knee or crouch down on one knee if they are

still standing. Repeat until everyone (except, of course, the leader) is an 'alien' and is sitting on the floor because they have made three mistakes (crouching on one knee for the first mistake, both knees for the second, finally sitting on the floor for the third).

3 'Slapping Hands': Kneel in a circle and place the left hand, palm down, in front of you; place your right hand to right of the next person's left hand, so that everyone's hands are crossing the hands of the people next to them, all around circle. Send a slap around the circle to the right, from left hand to left hand! Repeat, still sending the slap to the right, but this time from right hand to right hand. Then try sending the slaps in the opposite direction, to the left. (This warm-up requires patience and skill!).

12 Rhyming and nonsense play

1 'I did not go to school, because ...' Everyone thinks of the silliest reason, such as: 'I met a bulldozer on the way'; 'it was raining ice cream'; or 'it was Sunday anyway'.

2 'We cannot play football, because ...' Possible endings: 'they have planted potatoes on the pitch'; 'the guinea pig ate the football'; or 'they are playing hockey instead'.

3 In pairs, one person mimes a job and the other asks, 'What are you doing?' The answer should not fit the mime, for example: the person miming is pretending to dig the garden, but they answer 'fixing the bike', 'mixing a cake', or 'blowing my nose'.

4 As above, but when the person 'digging' the garden gives their answer, their partner starts to mime what they have said. Using the example above, they might start to blow their nose.

5 As above, but the person who was 'digging' the garden responds by saying, 'Why are you going to sleep? I said I was blowing my nose.' Then they start a different nonsense dialogue, such as beginning with a mime of feeding the birds.

13 Games for improvisation

1 Run a three-legged race with a partner, without tying the ankles.

2 Create 'stepping stones' with pieces of newspaper. Everyone has to cross the 'river' or the 'chasm' beneath the 'stones' without tearing the paper. Elaborate by having two people moving from 'stone to stone' together.

3 The group pretend they are medical students, and someone comes to give them a talk on knitting.

4 The group pretend they are housewives and househusbands, and someone comes to give them a talk on brain surgery.

5 Two people are fruit and vegetable stallholders, and call out what they are selling and for what price; they try to compete with each other.

6 In pairs, one partner is a customer and the other is trying to show off all the best points of a car without knowing anything about them; the 'car salesman' has to bluff their way through.

7 In pairs, one person is a student and the other a physics teacher; in reality the 'physics teacher' is a piano teacher and knows nothing about physics.

8 In small groups, one person leads the others across different types of terrain, such as desert, rainforest, ice flow, stream, farmyard, and so on. The group members don't know what the terrain is, so they follow and then guess at the end.

9 Repeat, but this time the groups are on ice that is about to crack, or in a place where they can see that there will shortly be a landslide; tell the groups everyone has to move quickly and lightly.

All of these exercises can be developed into situations or stories. Many will become favourites to be repeated. Very importantly, group members will start to develop their own versions of the exercises.

Feelings to Express & Change

Write names of feelings and colour the leaves.

Feelings I want to express

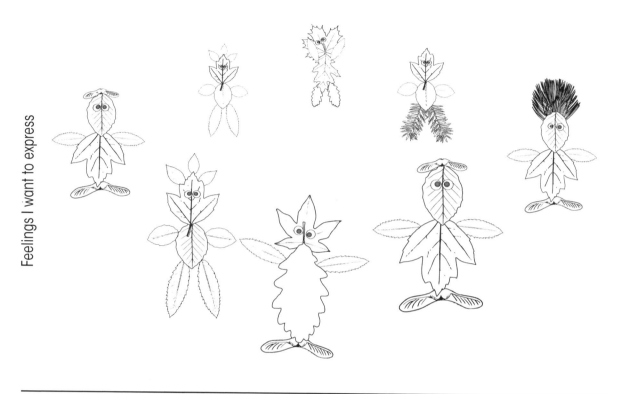

Feelings I want to change

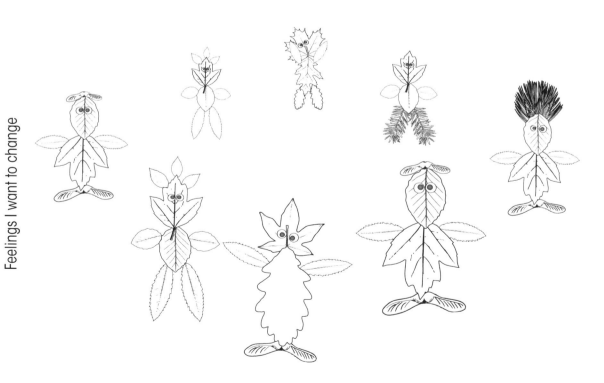

Actions that Show Feelings, & Change

Write names of actions and colour the leaves.

Actions that show my feelings

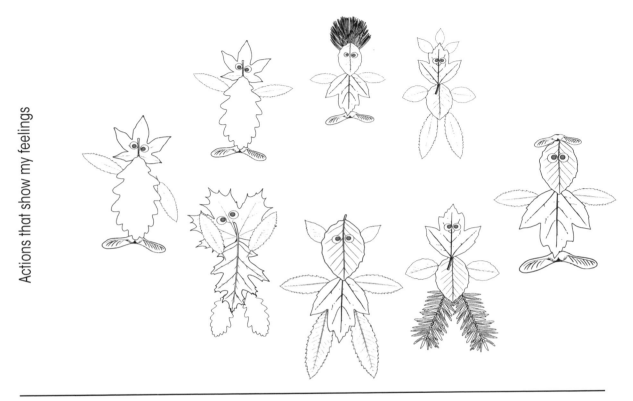

Actions that I would like to change

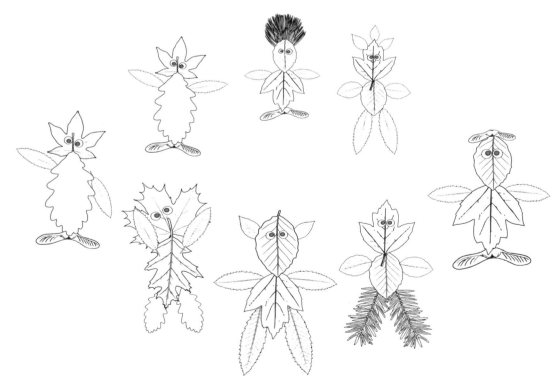

Decisions I Want to Make

Write your decisions and colour the leaves.

Distracting Sounds

Colour the picture in strong colours.

Draw or write the following:

Sounds that distract me are:

Sounds that help me focus are:

Distracting Sounds

Colour the picture in strong colours.

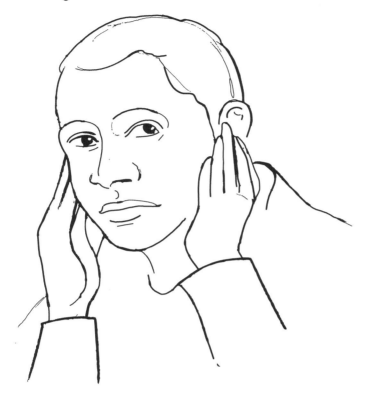

Draw or write the following:

Sounds that distract me are:

_____

Sounds that help me focus are:

Distracting Smells

Colour the picture in strong colours.

Draw or write the following:

Smells that distract me are:

_____

Smells that help me focus are:

Distracting Smells

Colour the picture in strong colours.

Draw or write the following:

Smells that distract me are:

_____

Smells that help me focus are:

Distracting Sights

Colour the picture in strong colours.

Draw or write the following:

Things I see that distract me are:

_____

Things I see that help me focus are:

Distracting Sights

Colour the picture in strong colours.

Draw or write the following:

Things I see that distract me are:

_____

Things I see that help me focus are:

WORKSHEET 6b: ACTIVITY 29

Distracting Memories

Colour the picture in strong colours.

Draw or write the following:

Memories that distract me are:

Memories that help me focus are:

Distracting Memories

Colour the picture in strong colours.

Draw or write the following:

Memories that distract me are:

_____

Memories that help me focus are:

Distracting Fears

Colour the picture in strong colours.

Draw or write the following:

Scary thoughts that distract me are:

Positive thoughts that help me focus are:

Distracting Fears

Colour the picture in strong colours.

Draw or write the following:

Scary thoughts that distract me are:

_____

Positive thoughts that help me focus are:

Distracting Worries

Colour the picture in strong colours.

Draw or write the following:

Worries that distract me are:

Actions to help me focus are:

Distracting Worries

Colour the picture in strong colours.

Draw or write the following:

Worries that distract me are:

_____

Actions to help me focus are:

Distracting Feelings

Colour the picture in strong colours.

Draw or write the following:

Feelings that distract me are:

_____

Feelings that help me focus are:

Distracting Feelings

Colour the picture in strong colours.

Draw or write the following:

Feelings that distract me are:

_____

Feelings that help me focus are:

WORKSHEET 10b: ACTIVITY 36

Distracting Disappointments

Colour the picture in strong colours.

Draw or write the following:

Disappointments that distract me are:

_____

Positive wishes that help me focus are:

Distracting Disappointments

Colour the picture in strong colours.

Draw or write the following:

Disappointments that distract me are:

_____

Positive wishes that help me focus are:

Colour the picture in strong colours.

Draw or write the following:

Excitements that distract me are:

Excitements that help me focus are:

Distracting Excitements

Colour the picture in strong colours.

Draw or write the following:

Excitements that distract me are:

_____

Excitements that help me focus are:

The Heart Tree

Colour the heart tree and write names or initials in the hearts if you wish.

Activities I Enjoy: Sport

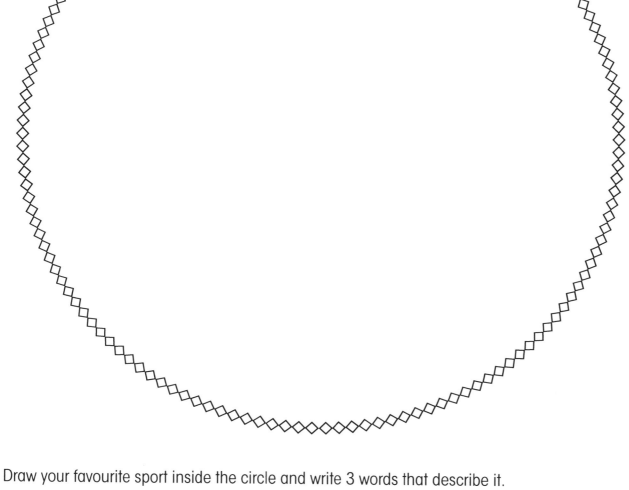

Draw your favourite sport inside the circle and write 3 words that describe it.

_____

_____

_____

Sports & Games:
Tug of Rope

Sports & Games: Swinging & Running

Sports & Games: Football & Rugby

Activities I Enjoy: Collections

Draw anything you like collecting inside the circle and write 3 words describe it.

_____

_____

_____

Template for Dice

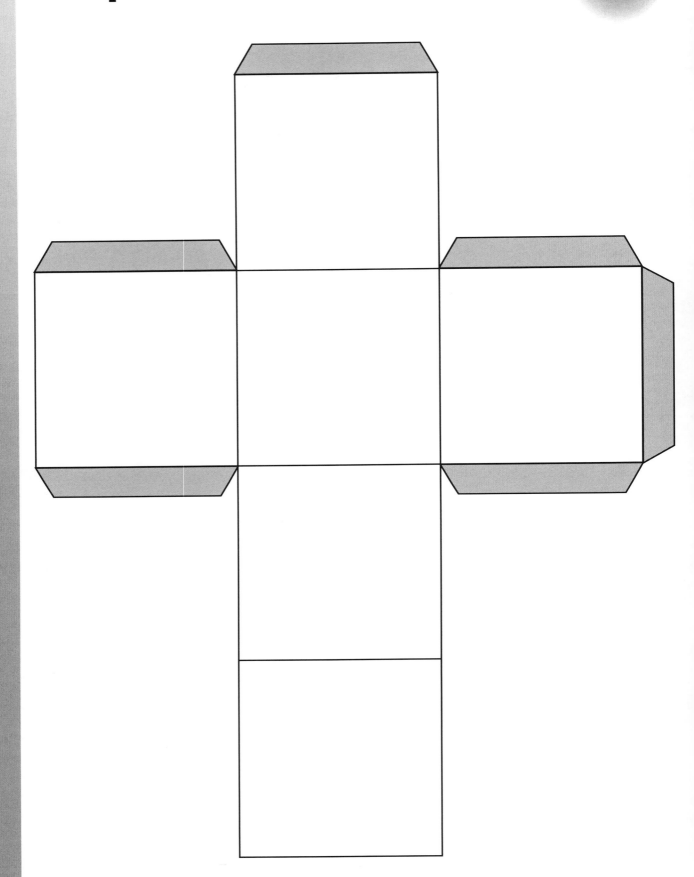

Group Contract & Agreement

We are attending the group on the following dates:

_____

We have not all chosen to be here.

Some of us have been asked to be in this group.

We all agree to abide by the group rules as follows:

1 Everyone listens to what other people are saying without interrupting.

2 Everyone agrees to behave in a respectful manner to others.

3 Everyone agrees that there is no verbal or physical violence.

4 Everyone agrees that equipment is not to be broken.

5 _____

6 _____

7 _____

Signature or Thumb Print from all Group Members:

Certificate of Achievement
Awarded to

_____

has shown skills in the following areas:

_____

_____

and has contributed to the group by:

_____

_____

_____   _____
Signed   Date

The Story of A Midsummer Night's Dream by William Shakespeare

The play is about three groups of people who interact with each other in various ways: the people of the court, the spirits of the forest and the workmen from the market in Athens.

There are arguments about who shall marry who in the court family, with Hermia wanting to marry Lysander and her father says she must marry Demetrius. Duke Theseus intervenes and says everyone must wait until his own wedding to Hippolyta. Hermia and Lysander decide to run away to the forest, and Helena tells Demetrius who immediately decides to pursue them!

Meanwhile there are arguments between the King and Queen of the Fairy Kingdom, Oberon and Titania. Oberon wants the little Indian boy that Titania has adopted, so everyone is bickering. Oberon calls his trusted servant Puck, who is always making mischief and practical jokes, and asks him to fetch a special flower that will make someone fall in love with the first creature they see on waking, when it is applied to their eyes.

There is a group of workman who are rehearsing a play that they want to perform at Duke Theseus wedding celebrations. They provide a lot of humour, especially when Bottom has a magical donkey's head put on him by Puck, and Titania wakes up and falls in love with him.

Everyone is challenging everyone else and Demetrius and Lysander want to fight as now they are both in love with Helens. Hermia wants to fight Helena because she thinks she has stolen her boyfriend. Oberon is punishing Titania because he wants the little boy.

The forest is a place of chaos but in the end everything works out. The lovers marry the people they want, Oberon and Titania resolve their differences, the weddings of all three couples go ahead, and the workmen perform their play.

The fairies give their blessings that all will be well.

(for an easy to understand edition of the play look at *No Fear Shakespeare: A Midsummer Night's Dream* published by Spark Publishing).

The Shepherd Boy &
the Weaving Maiden

In ancient times there was
a shepherd boy who lived with his poor family.

He went to work for a farmer and looked after his cow. The cow grew large and grew shining golden hair. One day the cow spoke in a human voice and said 'Today is the seventh day and the Jade Emperor's nine daughters will be bathing in the Sea of Heaven. You must take the clothes of the seventh daughter and ask her to marry you. She is the patron of the earthly weavers.' He replied, 'But she lives in the sky how can I reach her?'

The Golden Cow said that he should climb on her back and she would take him there. As he sat on her back, clouds spurted from her hoofs and she flew through the air and came to a stop by a beautiful garden with exquisite trees and flowers, and a large blue sea. There were rainbow-coloured birds singing in harmony and golden fish darting amongst the waves.

The Golden Cow said, 'Take the red clothes and hide in the trees, then ask her to marry you, and she can have her clothes back.' The Shepherd did as she asked, and the seventh daughter stayed crouching in the sea, pleading for her clothes. 'I have to ask my father', she said, but the Cow replied that she could arrange everything.

And so they were married and were very joyous, but after seven days the Weaving Maiden said she had to return to the palace and see to her weaving matters. She ran away and he pursued her: as he got nearer she took a needle from her hair and drew a line between them. The line became the Silver River, what we know as the Milky Way.

And now the Shepherd Boy and the Weaving Maiden can only meet once a year on the seventh day. All the crows from the skies create a bridge, wing to wing, so they can meet together and touch their hands. The Chinese say that it always rains on the seventh day as the tears fall from the young couple at their sadness of parting.

But their special day every year is filled with joy and gladness.

The Broken Promise: The Mulberry Tree

1. *Think about all the characters in the story and write or draw about one of them.*

In ancient times there was a family who lived on a farm where they had a large mulberry tree where the silk worms fed and eventually made beautiful silk. There was a grandmother, mother and father and a beautiful daughter. They also owned a very fine horse.

There was a sudden shock one day when the father was kidnapped by bandits who demanded a large ransom for his return. The family was very upset and cried for days, not knowing how to get him back. One day the mother was heard to say 'Whoever rescues my husband can have my daughter's hand in marriage!'

The horse, standing near the open window, heard this, and with a toss of his mane, galloped away towards the forest.

The next day the horse returned with the father on his back and everyone rejoiced. They held a fine feast to celebrate to welcome him home.

2. *Think of a broken promise and draw what happened. Does it still matter?*

Soon there was a banging on the door: it was the horse using his hoof, coming to claim his bride. The mother told her husband what she had promised and he got up and opened the door; then he shouted very loudly at the horse and sent him away.

That evening the daughter went to look at the mulberry tree to make sure it was fine, and then she went to the stable to talk to the horse. She stroked him very tenderly.

Suddenly there was a whoosh, and she was on the horse's back, as it galloped away, growing wings as it took to the skies. Later that evening her mother, father and grandmother went into the garden to look for her. As they looked up at the stars, there she was with the horse, waving to them.

'Don't worry about me, you will always see me when the moon is full and there are flowers on the Mulberry Tree. I have become the Goddess of Silk and Mulberry Trees'.

STORY SHEET 3

References & Further Reading

Bowlby J., 1965, *Child Care and the Growth of Love*, Pelican, London.

Bruner J. *et al.*, 1985, *Play: Its Role in Development and Evolution*, Penguin, London.

Chambers (ed.), 2008, *Chambers Rhyming Dictionary*, 2nd edn, Chambers Harrap Publishers Ltd., Edinburgh.

Corbett P. & Thomson R., 2003, *Black's Rhyming and Spelling Dictionary*, A.&C. Black Publishers Ltd., London.

Hunter K., 2014, *Shakespeare's Heartbeat: Drama Games for Children with Autism*, Routledge, Hove.

Jennings S., 1990, *Dramatherapy with Families, Groups and Individuals*, Jessica Kingsley Publishers, London.

Jennings S., 1998, *Introduction to Dramatherapy: Ariadne's Ball of Thread*, Jessica Kingsley Publishers London.

Jennings S., 1999, *Introduction to Developmental Play Therapy*, Jessica Kingsley Publishers, London.

Jennings S., 2011, *Healthy Attachments and Neuro-Dramatic-Play*, Jessica Kingsley Publishers, London.

Jennings S., 2011, *101 Activities for Empathy & Awareness*, Hinton House Publishers, Buckingham.

Jennings S., 2013, *101 Activities for Social & Emotional Resilience*, Hinton House Publishers, Buckingham.

Jennings S., 2013, *101 Ideas for Managing Challenging Behaviour*, Hinton House Publishers, Buckingham.

Jennings S., 2014, *101 Ideas for Positive Thoughts and Feelings*, Hinton House Publishers, Buckingham.

McFarlane P., 2005, *Dramatherapy: Developing Emotional Stability*, David Fulton Publishers Ltd., London.

McFarlane P., 2012, *Creative Drama for Emotional Support: Activities and Exercises for Use in the Classroom*, Jessica Kingsley Publishers, London.

Newham P., 1999, *The Healing Voice*, Vega Books, London.

Seligman M., 2011, *Flourish: A New Understanding of Happiness and Well-Being*, Nicholas Brealey Publishing, London.

Sutton-Smith B., 2001, *The Ambiguity of Play*, First Harvard University Press, Harvard, Mass.

Recommended Resources

Rogerson H., 2014, *How's My World? Feelings and Emotions Cards*, Hinton House Publishers, Buckingham.

Rory's Story Cubes: Original, 2010, The Creativity Hub, Belfast.

Rory's Story Cubes: Actions, 2010, The Creativity Hub, Belfast.

101 Activities & Ideas

* Creative and practical solutions to issues around emotional well-being in young people. Many teachers, care workers and therapists are challenged by difficult behaviours, and families often feel lost for solutions to sudden outbursts or young people's feelings of alienation and lack of self-esteem.

* Containing a host of ideas for home, school and youth groups, the books will help to tackle these difficult issues in a positive and active way. There are no magic answers, but the ideas aim to empower young people to find solutions to some of their own difficulties, while providing guidance for more positive directions.

* The books adopt a 'hands-on' approach with a firm and enabling attitude and provide a sound practical basis for active intervention for behaviour change.

101 Activities for Empathy & Awareness
ISBN: 978-1-906531-33-1

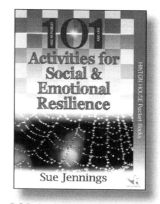

101 Activities for Social & Emotional Resilience
ISBN: 978-1-906531-46-1

101 Ideas for Managing Challenging Behaviour
ISBN: 978-1-906531-44-7

101 Activities for Increasing Focus & Motivation
ISBN: 978-1-906531-45-4

101 Ideas for Positive Thoughts & Feelings
ISBN: 978-1-906531-47-8

 www.hintonpublishers.com

The 50 Best Games series ...

☀ These handy pocket books will ensure you are never again stuck for activity ideas that will help make both teaching and learning fun!

☀ Carefully selected, each collection of the 50 Best Games is themed and addresses a specific area of development. All the games are easy to implement with the minimum of preparation and can be adapted to the needs of your particular group.

☀ Use them as warm-ups, ice breakers, time fillers or to address a specific need. Suitable for groups of all sizes and can be used with all ages from young children to adolescents.

The 50 Best Games for Building Self-Esteem

ISBN 978-0-906531-18-8

The 50 Best Perception Games

ISBN 978-0-906531-11-9

The 50 Best Games for Brain Exercise

ISBN 978-0-906531-14-0

The 50 Best Games for Relaxation & Concentration

ISBN 978-0-906531-17-1

The 50 Best Games for Speech & Language Development

ISBN 978-0-906531-13-3

The 50 Best Games for Children's Groups

ISBN 978-0-906531-12-6

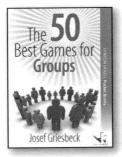

The 50 Best Games for Groups

ISBN 978-0-906531-16-4

The 50 Best Indoor Games for Groups

ISBN 978-0-906531-15-7

www.hintonpublishers.com